May 2014

Dear Barb,

   Thank you for pursuing beauty... in your gardens and window boxes

   ... in your creation of your own cards and calligraphy to bless others

   ... in teaching others to garden and sharing plant starts

   ... in planting seeds in hearts and lives of others
   — seeds of kindness and seeds of Jesus' love

   ... in your art and painting!

   One of your friends,
   Peg

TO

Barb

FROM

Peggy

Then God saw everything
that He had made,
and indeed it was very good.
—
Genesis 1:31 NKJV

A Gardener's
LITTLE
DEVOTIONAL
BOOK

Copyright © 2014 by Worthy Inspired, a division of Worthy Media, Inc.

ISBN 978-1-60587-561-3
ISBN 978-1-60587-572-9 (Special Edition)

Published by Worthy Inspired, a division of Worthy Media, Inc.,
134 Franklin Road, Suite 200, Brentwood, Tennessee 37027.

Scripture references marked KJV are from the Holy Bible, King James Version

Scripture references marked NKJV are from the Holy Bible, New King James Version. Copyright © 1982 by Thomas Nelson, Inc. Used by permission.

Scripture references marked NCV are from the New Century Version®. Copyright © 1987, 1988, 1991 by Word Publishing, a division of Thomas Nelson, Inc. All rights reserved. Used by permission.

Scripture references marked HCSB are from the Holman Christian Standard Bible™ Copyright © 1999, 2000, 2001 by Holman Bible Publishers. Used by permission.

Scripture references marked NIV are from the Holy Bible, New International Version®. Copyright © 1973, 1978, 1984 International Bible Society. Used by permission of Zondervan. All rights reserved.

Scripture references marked NLT are from the Holy Bible. New Living Translation. Copyright © 1996 Tyndale Charitable Trust. Used by permission of Tyndale House Publishers.

Scripture references marked NASB are from the New American Standard Bible®. Copyright © 1960, 1962, 1963, 1968, 1971, 1972, 1973, 1975, 1977, 1995 by The Lockman Foundation. Used by permission.

Scripture references marked MSG are from the Message. Copyright © 1993, 1994, 1995, 1996, 2000, 2001, 2002. Used by permission of NavPress Publishing Group.

Cover Design by Kim Russell / Wahoo Designs
Page Layout by Bart Dawson

Printed in the United States of America

1 2 3 4 5—RRD—18 17 16 15 14

A Gardener's LITTLE DEVOTIONAL BOOK

WORTHY
Inspired

Introduction

Whenever we pause to consider God's glorious universe, we marvel at the miracle of nature. The smallest seedlings and grandest stars are all part of God's infinite creation. God has placed His handiwork on display for all to see, and if we're wise, we make time each day to celebrate the world that surrounds us.

In the garden, we come face-to-face, nose-to-nose, and hand-to-hand with God's good earth. Thus, the garden is a perfect place to observe the Creator's work and to sense His presence.

This text contains 100 devotional readings for gardeners. These passages celebrate the glory of God's creation and the miracle of His unending love.

Success in the garden—or outside it—depends upon certain unchanging principles. So, if you're ready to get your hands dirty and dig for insights about land and life, turn the page. But before you do, give thanks to your Creator for all the opportunities He has given you—including, of course, the opportunity to tend a garden.

Say your prayers in a garden early,
ignoring steadfastly the dew, the birds
and the flowers, and you will come away
overwhelmed by its freshness and joy;
go there in order to be overwhelmed.

—

C. S. Lewis

God's Creation

And to every beast of the earth and to every bird of the sky and to every thing that moves on the earth which has life . . . God saw all that He had made, and behold, it was very good.

Genesis 1:30-31 NASB

The observant gardener witnesses a show like no other. And the price of admission is indeed a bargain: a plot of ground, a ray of hope, and a handful of seeds.

Today presents another opportunity to celebrate God's handiwork. Will you join in the celebration? If you are wise, you will pause and examine the exquisite details of God's glorious creation. When you do, you'll discover that the more carefully you inspect God's unfolding universe, the more beautiful it becomes.

Sometimes, a garden can be a frustrating place. Plants can be stubborn, pests can be persistent, and weather can be uncooperative. When things begin to grow wrong, so do emotions—but no one should work the soil in anger.

So the next time you find yourself muttering about weeds, weather, or bugs, pause to give thanks for your garden; it's a gift from God that keeps on giving—and as a gardener, you're strongly advised to keep on thanking Him for that gift.

No philosophical theory which I have yet come across is a radical improvement on the words of Genesis, that "in the beginning God made Heaven and Earth."

C. S. Lewis

To create a little flower is the labor of ages.

William Blake

Today, you will encounter God's creation. When you see the beauty around you, let each detail remind you to lift your head in praise.

Max Lucado

A HEALTHY THOUGHT FOR GARDENERS

God writes the gospel not in the Bible alone, but on the trees, and flowers, and clouds, and stars.

Martin Luther

A GARDENER'S PRAYER

Dear Lord, You have created a world that is glorious to behold yet impossible to comprehend. I praise You for Your creation, Father, and for the sense of awe and wonder that You have placed in my heart. Today, as I venture out to my garden, I will pause to admire Your handiwork. This is the day that You have made, and I will rejoice in it. Amen

The Joys of Gardening

The LORD is king! Let the earth rejoice! Let the farthest islands be glad.

Psalm 97:1 NLT

Gardening, if done properly, is a joyful pursuit. Whether it's a big two-acre spread or a tiny midtown window box, a garden is a place where the majesty of nature is revealed each day.

As the seasons pass and the cycle of life unfolds, thoughtful gardeners (like you) pause to reflect upon the infinite power of the Creator and the infinite value of His creation.

Joy, whether in the garden or outside it, is a choice. How will you choose?

C. H. Spurgeon, the renowned 19th-century English clergyman, could have been talking about a garden gate when he advised, "The Lord is glad to open the gate to every knocking soul. It opens very freely; its hinges are not rusted; no bolts secure it. Have faith and enter at this moment through holy courage. If you knock with a heavy heart, you shall yet sing with joy of spirit. Never be discouraged!"

If, today, your heart is heavy, open the door of your soul to Christ. He will give you peace and joy. And, if you already have the joy of Christ in your heart, share it freely, just as Christ freely shared His joy with you.

When we get rid of inner conflicts and wrong attitudes toward life, we will almost automatically burst into joy.

E. Stanley Jones

Joy is the direct result of having God's perspective on our daily lives and the effect of loving our Lord enough to obey His commands and trust His promises.

Bill Bright

You have to look for the joy. Look for the light of God that is hitting your life, and you will find sparkles you didn't know were there.

Barbara Johnson

A HEALTHY THOUGHT FOR GARDENERS

How fair is a garden amid the toils and passions of existence.

Benjamin Disraeli

A GARDENER'S PRAYER

Dear Lord, when I am working in the garden—and when I am not—I will choose to be a joyful Christian. You have given me countless blessings, and I will celebrate Your gifts. I will make Your joy my joy. I will praise Your works, I will obey Your Word, and I will honor Your Son, this day and every day of my life. Amen

This Is His Day

This is the day the LORD has made. We will rejoice and be glad in it.

Psalm 118:24 NLT

A visit to the garden should be a cause for celebration. Do you feel like celebrating? Hopefully so. After all, this day—and every day—is a blessed gift from God.

God gives us this day; He fills it to the brim with possibilities, and He challenges us to use it for His purposes. The day is presented to us fresh and clean at midnight, free of charge, but we must beware: Today is a non-renewable resource—once it's gone, it's gone forever. Our responsibility, of course, is to use this day in the service of God's will and according to His commandments.

Today, whether you're spending happy moments in the garden or not, treasure the time that God has given you. Give Him the glory and the praise and the thanksgiving that He deserves. And search for the hidden possibilities that God has placed along your path. This day is a priceless gift from God, so use it joyfully and encourage others to do likewise. After all, this is the day the Lord has made....

A life of intimacy with God is characterized by joy.

Oswald Chambers

All our life is a celebration for us; we are convinced, in fact, that God is always everywhere. We sing while we work… we pray while we carry out all life's other occupations.

St. Clement of Alexandria

If you can forgive the person you were, accept the person you are, and believe in the person you will become, you are headed for joy. So celebrate your life.

Barbara Johnson

Some of us seem so anxious about avoiding hell that we forget to celebrate our journey toward heaven.

Philip Yancey

A TIP FROM THE GARDEN

Health, wealth, and happiness will come forth from the earth if we diligently work for the harvest.

Jim G. Brown

A GARDENER'S PRAYER

Dear Lord, today I will celebrate Your gifts. Whether I'm in the garden or not—whether I'm celebrating a great victory or enduring an unwelcome disappointment—I will be a joyful Christian, a worthy example to others, and a dutiful servant to You. Amen

Not Enough Hours?

It is good to give thanks to the Lord, to sing praises to the Most High. It is good to proclaim your unfailing love in the morning, your faithfulness in the evening.

Psalm 92:1-2 NLT

Like a successful garden, a faithful heart must be tended with care. And, a wonderful way to tend to your spiritual needs is to spend a few precious minutes each morning with your heavenly Father.

If you ever find that you're simply "too busy" for a daily chat with God, it's time to take a long, hard look at your priorities and your values. Each day has 1,440 minutes—do you value your relationship with God enough to spend a few of those minutes with Him? He deserves that much of your time and more—is He receiving it from you? Hopefully so.

As you consider your plans for the day ahead, here's a tip: organize your life around this simple principle: "God first." When you place your Creator where He belongs—at the very center of your day and your life—the rest of your priorities will fall into place.

A person with no devotional life generally struggles with faith and obedience.

Charles Stanley

This day's bustle and hurly-burly would too often and too soon call us away from Jesus' feet. These distractions must be immediately dismissed, or we shall know only the "barrenness of busyness."

A. W. Tozer

The busier we are, the easier it is to worry, the greater the temptation to worry, the greater the need to be alone with God.

Charles Stanley

There is an enormous power in little things to distract our attention from God.

Oswald Chambers

A HEALTHY THOUGHT FOR GARDENERS

God is an artist, and the universe is His work of art.

Thomas Aquinas

A GARDENER'S PRAYER

Dear Lord, every day of my life is a journey with You. I will take time today to think, to pray, and to study Your Word. Guide my steps, Father, and keep me mindful that today offers yet another opportunity to celebrate Your blessings, Your love, and Your Son. Amen

Cultivating an Attitude of Gratitude

Finally brothers, whatever is true, whatever is honorable, whatever is just, whatever is pure, whatever is lovely, whatever is commendable—if there is any moral excellence and if there is any praise—dwell on these things.

Philippians 4:8 HCSB

Thoughts, like gardens, can be carefully cultivated . . . or not. How will you direct your thoughts today? Will you obey the words of Philippians 4:8 by dwelling upon those things that are honorable, just, and commendable? Or will you allow your thoughts to be hijacked by the negativity that seems to dominate our troubled world? Are you fearful, angry, bored, or worried? Are you so preoccupied with the concerns of this day that you fail to thank God for the promise of eternity? Are you confused, bitter, or pessimistic? If so, God wants to have a little talk with you.

God intends that you experience joy and abundance. So, today and every day hereafter, celebrate the life that God has given you by focusing your thoughts upon those things that are worthy of praise. Today, count your blessings instead of your hardships. And thank the Giver of all things good for gifts that are simply too numerous to count.

The mind is like a clock that is constantly running down. It has to be wound up daily with good thoughts.

Fulton J. Sheen

"If the Lord will" is not just a statement on a believer's lips; it is the constant attitude of his heart.

Warren Wiersbe

The life of strain is difficult. The life of inner peace—a life that comes from a positive attitude—is the easiest type of existence.

Norman Vincent Peale

All things being equal, attitude wins. All things not being equal, attitude sometimes still wins.

John Maxwell

A HEALTHY THOUGHT FOR GARDENERS

Good thoughts bear good fruit and bad thoughts bear bad fruit. And a man is his own gardener.

James Allen

A GARDENER'S PRAYER

Dear Lord, help me cultivate an attitude that is pleasing to You as I count my blessings today, tomorrow, and every day. Amen

Giving Thanks for God's Abundance

I have come that they may have life, and that they may have it more abundantly.

John 10:10 NKJV

The abundant life, like a beautiful garden, is a gift from above. God bestows that gift upon those of us who are wise enough to accept it.

The 10th chapter of John tells us that Christ came to earth so that our lives might be filled with abundance. But what, exactly, did Jesus mean when He promised "life . . . more abundantly"? Was He referring to material possessions or financial wealth? Hardly. Jesus offers a different kind of abundance: a spiritual richness that extends beyond the temporal boundaries of this world. This everlasting abundance is available to all who seek it and claim it. May we, as believers, claim the riches of Christ Jesus every day that we live, and may we share His blessings with all who cross our path.

The only way you can experience abundant life is to surrender your plans to Him.

Charles Stanley

If you want purpose and meaning and satisfaction and fulfillment and peace and hope and joy and abundant life that lasts forever, look to Jesus.

Anne Graham Lotz

Jesus wants Life for us, Life with a capital L.

John Eldredge

I believe God intended for everybody to have at least one acre. Of course, He expects us to labor six days each week if we are to prosper thereon.

Jim G. Brown

A TIP FROM THE GARDEN

It is great—and there is no other greatness—to make one nook of God's creation more fruitful.

Thomas Carlyle

A GARDENER'S PRAYER

Dear Lord, You have offered me the gift of abundance through Your Son. Thank You, Father, for the abundant life that is mine through Christ Jesus. Let me accept His gifts and use them always to glorify You. Amen

The Power of Prayer

The intense prayer of the righteous is very powerful.

James 5:16 HCSB

Prayer is a powerful tool for communicating with our Creator; it is an opportunity to commune with the Giver of all things good. "The power of prayer": these words are so familiar, yet sometimes we forget what they mean. Prayer helps us find strength for today and hope for the future. Prayer is not a thing to be taken lightly or to be used infrequently.

The quality of your spiritual life will be in direct proportion to the quality of your prayer life. Prayer changes things, and it changes you. Today, instead of turning things over in your mind, turn them over to God in prayer. Instead of worrying about your next decision, ask God to lead the way. Pray constantly about things great and small. God is listening, and He wants to hear from you now.

Where there is much prayer, there will be much of the Spirit; where there is much of the Spirit, there will be ever-increasing power.

Andrew Murray

Prayer is the most important tool for your mission to the world. People may refuse our love or reject our message, but they are defenseless against our prayers.

Rick Warren

Is prayer your steering wheel or your spare tire?

Corrie ten Boom

God delights in the prayers of His children—prayers that express our love for Him, prayers that share our deepest burdens with Him.

Billy Graham

A HEALTHY THOUGHT FOR GARDENERS

When we who have a feeling for birds observe a mighty eagle, or the perfection of a tiny warbler, we see, not the inspiration of God filtered through human agency, but the very handiwork of the Creator Himself.

Rosalie Edge

A GARDENER'S PRAYER

Dear Lord, let me raise my hopes and my dreams, my worries and my fears to You. Let me be a worthy example to family and friends, showing them the importance and the power of prayer. Let me take everything to You in prayer, Lord, and when I do, let me trust in Your answers. Amen

Giving Thanks for Today's Opportunities

When we were baptized, we were buried with Christ and shared his death. So, just as Christ was raised from the dead by the wonderful power of the Father, we also can live a new life.

Romans 6:4 NCV

Each morning offers a fresh opportunity to invite Christ, yet once again, to rule over our hearts and our days. Each morning provides another opportunity to sow seeds of hope among our family and friends. Each morning presents yet another chance to take up His cross and follow in His footsteps.

God's Word is clear: When we genuinely invite Him to reign over our hearts, and when we accept His transforming love, we are forever changed. When we welcome Christ into our hearts, an old life ends and a new way of living—along with a completely new way of viewing the world—begins.

Today, let us rejoice in the new life that is ours through Christ, and let us follow Him, step by step, on the path that He first walked.

Turn your life over to Christ today, and your life will never be the same.

Billy Graham

No man is ever the same after God has laid His hand upon him.

A. W. Tozer

The transforming love of God has repositioned me for eternity. I am now a new man, forgiven, basking in the warm love of our living God, trusting His promises and provision, and enjoying life to the fullest.

Bill Bright

A HEALTHY THOUGHT FOR GARDENERS

Flowers are the sweetest things God ever made and forgot to put a soul into.

Henry Ward Beecher

A GARDENER'S PRAYER

Heavenly Father, renew in me the passion to share the Good News of Jesus Christ. Make the experience of my conversion real and fresh so that I might be an effective witness for You. Amen

Beyond Worry

Blessed is he that trusts in the Lord.

Proverbs 16:20 NIV

Because we are imperfect human beings, we worry. Even though we are Christians who have been given the assurance of salvation—even though we are Christians who have received the promise of God's love and protection—we find ourselves fretting over the countless details of everyday life. Jesus understood our concerns when He spoke the reassuring words found in Matthew 6: "Therefore I tell you, do not worry about your life . . ."

As you consider the promises of Jesus, remember that God still sits in His heaven and you are His beloved child. Then, whether you're tending your garden or tending to the obligations of everyday life, you can worry less and trust God more. And that's as it should be because God is trustworthy . . . and you are protected.

It is not work that's kills, but worry. And, it is amazing how much wear and tear the human mind and spirit can stand if it is free from friction and well-oiled by the Spirit.

Vance Havner

We are not called to be burden-bearers, but cross-bearers and light-bearers. We must cast our burdens on the Lord.

Corrie ten Boom

I've read the last page of the Bible. It's all going to turn out all right.

Billy Graham

It has been well said that no man ever sank under the burden of the day. It is when tomorrow's burden is added to the burden of today that the weight is more than a man can bear. Never load yourselves so, my friends. If you find yourselves so loaded, at least remember this: it is your own doing, not God's. He begs you to leave the future to Him and mind the present.

George MacDonald

A HEALTHY THOUGHT FOR GARDENERS

Cares melt when you kneel in your garden.

Old Saying

A GARDENER'S PRAYER

Forgive me, Lord, when I worry. Worry reflects a lack of trust in You. Help me to work, Lord, and not to worry. And, keep me mindful, Father, that nothing, absolutely nothing, will happen this day that You and I cannot handle together. Amen

Cultivating a Strong Faith

For whatever is born of God overcomes the world. And this is the victory that has overcome the world—our faith.

1 John 5:4 NKJV

The first element of a successful garden or a successful life is faith: faith in the future, faith in God, faith in His Son, and faith in His promises. If we place our lives in God's hands, our faith is rewarded in ways that we—as human beings with clouded vision and limited understanding—can scarcely comprehend. But, if we seek to rely solely upon our own resources, or if we seek earthly success outside the boundaries of God's commandments, we reap a bitter harvest for ourselves and for our loved ones.

Trust God today and every day that you live. Then, when you have entrusted your future to the Giver of all things good, rest assured that your future is secure, not only for today, but also for all eternity.

Faith does not concern itself with the entire journey. One step is enough.

Mrs. Charles E. Cowman

Just as our faith strengthens our prayer life, so do our prayers deepen our faith. Let us pray often, starting today, for a deeper, more powerful faith.

Shirley Dobson

Faith, as Paul saw it, was a living, flaming thing leading to surrender and obedience to the commandments of Christ.

A. W. Tozer

Faith is seeing light with the eyes of your heart, when the eyes of your body see only darkness.

Barbara Johnson

A TIP FROM THE GARDEN

To cultivate a garden is to walk with God.

Christain Bovee

A GARDENER'S PRAYER

Father, in the dark moments of my life, help me remember that You are always near and that You can overcome any challenge. Keep me mindful of Your love and Your power, so that I may live courageously and faithfully today and every day. Amen

Our Greatest Refuge

For you have need of endurance, so that when you have done the will of God, you may receive what was promised.

Hebrews 10:36 NASB

G od is our greatest refuge. When every earthly support system fails, God remains steadfast, and His love remains unchanged. When we encounter life's inevitable disappointments and setbacks, God remains faithful. When we suffer losses that leave us breathless, God is always with us, always ready to respond to our prayers, always working in us and through us to turn tragedy into triumph.

Author and speaker Patsy Clairmont observed, "If you are walking toward Jesus to the best of your ability, he will see you through life's unpredictable waters—but you must risk launching the boat." And that's sound advice because even during life's most difficult days, God stands by us. Our job, of course, is to return the favor and stand by Him.

Whether our fear is absolutely realistic or out of proportion in our minds, our greatest refuge is Jesus Christ.

Luci Swindoll

I am grateful that when even a single sparrow falls the ground, God knows—and understands.

Ruth Bell Graham

Our future may look fearfully intimidating, yet we can look up to the Engineer of the Universe, confident that nothing escapes His attention or slips out of the control of those strong hands.

Elisabeth Elliot

God will never let you sink under your circumstances. He always provides a safety net and His love always encircles.

Barbara Johnson

A TIP FROM THE GARDEN

The first rule of successful gardening is to work with, not against, the natural setting.

Burpee Complete Gardener

A GARDENER'S PRAYER

Lord, You are my Shepherd. You care for me; You comfort me; You watch over me; and You have saved me. I will praise You, Father, for Your glorious works, for Your protection, for Your love, and for Your Son. Amen

In Times of Adversity

For whatever is born of God overcomes the world. And this is the victory that has overcome the world—our faith.

1 John 5:4 NKJV

Sometimes, our harvests are bountiful; sometimes they are not. But during life's darker days, there is a source of strength upon which we, as Christians, must depend.

In times of trouble, God stands ready to protect us. Our responsibility, of course, is to ask Him for protection. When we do, He hears our prayers, and He answers those prayers in His own way and in His own time.

Are you worried or confused? Does your future seem foreboding? Are you anxious about your finances, your health, or your relationships? If so, you must turn your concerns over to a power far greater than your own.

Whether your harvest is bountiful or not, lift your prayers to the Father whose love for you is infinite and eternal. He will never fail you.

God will not permit any troubles to come upon us unless He has a specific plan by which great blessing can come out of the difficulty.

Peter Marshall

Adversity is always unexpected and unwelcomed. It is an intruder and a thief, and yet in the hands of God, adversity becomes the means through which His supernatural power is demonstrated.

Charles Stanley

Tribulation is a gift from God—one that He especially gives His special friends.

St. Thomas More

God will make obstacles serve His purpose.

Mrs. Charles E. Cowman

A TIP FROM THE GARDEN

The fair-weather gardener, who will do nothing except when the wind and weather and everything else are favorable, is never a master of his craft.

Henry Ellacombe

A GARDENER'S PRAYER

Dear Heavenly Father, when I am troubled, You heal me. When I am afraid, You protect me. When I am discouraged, You lift me up. In times of adversity, let me trust Your plan and Your will for my life. And whatever my circumstances, Lord, let me always give the thanks and the glory to You. Amen

Taking Up the Cross

Then He said to them all, "If anyone wants to come with Me, he must deny himself, take up his cross daily, and follow Me."

Luke 9:23 HCSB

When Jesus addressed His disciples, He warned them that each one must, "take up his cross daily and follow me" (Luke 9:23 NIV). Christ's message was clear: in order to follow Him, Christ's disciples must deny themselves and, instead, trust Him completely. Nothing has changed since then.

When we have been saved by Christ, we can, if we choose, become passive Christians. We can sit back, secure in our own salvation, and let other believers spread the healing message of Jesus. But to do so is wrong. Instead, we are commanded to become disciples of the One who has saved us.

Do you seek to fulfill God's purpose for your life? Then follow Christ. Follow Him by picking up His cross today and every day that you live. Then, you will quickly discover that Christ's love has the power to change everything, including you.

Discipleship means personal, passionate devotion to a Person, our Lord Jesus Christ.

Oswald Chambers

It is the secret of true discipleship to bear the cross, to acknowledge the death sentence that has been passed on self, and to deny any right that self has to rule over us.

Andrew Murray

There is not Christianity without a cross, for you cannot be a disciple of Jesus without taking up your cross.

Henry Blackaby

If we would be followers of Christ, indeed we must become personally and vitally involved in His death and resurrection. And this requires repentance, prayer, watchfulness, self-denial, detachment from the world, humility, obedience, and cross carrying.

A. W. Tozer

A TIP FROM THE GARDEN

Study nature as the countenance of God.

Charles Kingsley

A GARDENER'S PRAYER

Help me, Lord, to understand what cross I am to bear this day. Give me the strength and the courage to carry that cross along the path of Your choosing so that I may be a worthy disciple of Your Son. Amen

Asking for Directions

If you need wisdom—if you want to know what God wants you to do—ask him, and he will gladly tell you. He will not resent your asking.

James 1:5 NLT

Genuine, heartfelt prayer produces powerful changes in us and in our world. When we lift our hearts to God, we open ourselves to a never-ending source of divine wisdom and infinite love. Jesus made it clear to His disciples: they should petition God to meet their needs. So should we.

Do you have questions about your future that you simply can't answer? Do you have needs that you simply can't meet by yourself? Do you sincerely seek to know God's unfolding plans for your life? If so, ask Him for direction, for protection, and for strength—and then keep asking Him every day that you live. Whatever your need, no matter how great or small, pray about it and have faith. God is not just near; He is here, and He's perfectly capable of answering your prayers. Now, it's up to you to ask.

Notice that we must ask. And we will sometimes struggle to hear and struggle with what we hear. But personally, it's worth it. I'm after the path of life—and he alone knows it.

John Eldredge

Aspire to God with short but frequent outpourings of the heart; admire His bounty; invoke His aid; cast yourself in spirit at the foot of His cross; adore His goodness; treat with Him of your salvation; give Him your whole soul a thousand times in the day.

St. Francis of Sales

We honor God by asking for great things when they are a part of His promise. We dishonor Him and cheat ourselves when we ask for molehills where He has promised mountains.

Vance Havner

A HEALTHY THOUGHT FOR GARDENERS

It's difficult to think anything but pleasant thoughts while eating a homegrown tomato.

Lewis Grizzard

A GARDENER'S PRAYER

Lord, when I have questions about my purpose in life, I will turn to You. When I am weak, I will seek Your strength. When I am discouraged, Father, I will be mindful of Your love and Your grace. I will ask You for the things I need, Father, and I will trust Your answers, today and forever. Amen

Courage for the Journey

But Jesus immediately said to them: "Take courage! It is I. Don't be afraid."

Matthew 14:27 NIV

A storm rose quickly on the Sea of Galilee, and the disciples were afraid. Although they had seen Jesus perform many miracles, the disciples feared for their lives, so they turned to their Savior, and He calmed the waters and the wind.

Sometimes, we, like the disciples, feel threatened by the inevitable storms of life. And when we are fearful, we, too, can turn to Christ for courage and for comfort.

The next time you're afraid, remember that the One who calmed the wind and the waves is also your personal Savior. And remember that the ultimate battle has already been won at Calvary. We, as believers, can live courageously in the promises of our Lord . . . and we should.

To fear and not be afraid, that is the paradox of faith.

A. W. Tozer

Down through the centuries, in times of trouble and trial, God has brought courage to the hearts of those who love Him. The Bible is filled with assurances of God's help and comfort in every kind of trouble.

Billy Graham

The fear of God is the death of every other fear.

C. H. Spurgeon

What is courage? It is the ability to be strong in trust, in conviction, in obedience. To be courageous is to step out in faith—to trust and obey, no matter what.

Kay Arthur

A HEALTHY THOUGHT FOR GARDENERS

Beauty may be said to be God's trademark in creation.

Henry Ward Beecher

A GARDENER'S PRAYER

Dear Lord, sometimes I face disappointments and challenges that leave me worried and afraid. When I am fearful, let me seek Your strength. Keep me mindful, Lord, that You are my God. With You by my side, Lord, I have nothing to fear. Help me to be Your grateful and courageous servant this day and every day. Amen

Giving Thanks for God's Guidance

The steps of the Godly are directed by God. He delights in every detail of their lives.

Psalm 37:22 NLT

God is intensely interested in each of us, and He will guide our steps if we serve Him obediently.

When we sincerely offer heartfelt prayers to our Heavenly Father, He will give direction and meaning to our lives—but He won't force us to follow Him. To the contrary, God has given us the free will to follow His commandments . . . or not.

When we stray from God's commandments, we invite bitter consequences. But, when we follow His commandments, and when we genuinely and humbly seek His will, He touches our hearts and leads us on the path of His choosing.

Will you trust God to guide your steps? You should. When you entrust your life to Him completely and without reservation, God will give you the strength to meet any challenge, the courage to face any trial, and the wisdom to live in His righteousness and in His peace. So trust Him today and seek His guidance. When you do, your next step will be the right one.

A spiritual discipline is necessary in order to move slowly from an absurd to an obedient life, from a life filled with noisy worries to a life in which there is some free inner space where we can listen to our God and follow his guidance.

Henri Nouwen

Men give advice; God gives guidance.

Leonard Ravenhill

I don't doubt that the Holy Spirit guides your decisions from within when you make them with the intention of pleasing God. The error would be to think that He speaks only within, whereas in reality He speaks also through Scripture, the Church, Christian friends, and books.

C. S. Lewis

A HEALTHY THOUGHT FOR GARDENERS

God almighty first planted a garden. And, indeed, it is the purest of human pleasures.

Francis Bacon

A GARDENER'S PRAYER

Dear Lord, You always stand ready to guide me. Let me accept Your guidance, today and every day of my life. Lead me, Father, so that my life can be a tribute to Your grace, to Your mercy, to Your love, and to Your Son. Amen

His Promises

Let's keep a firm grip on the promises that keep us going. He always keeps his word.

Hebrews 10:23 MSG

The Christian faith is founded upon promises that are contained in a unique book. That book is the Holy Bible. The Bible is a roadmap for life here on earth and for life eternal. As Christians, we are called upon to study its meaning, to trust its promises, to follow its commandments, and to share its Good News. God's Holy Word is, indeed, a transforming, life-changing, one-of-a-kind treasure. And, a passing acquaintance with the Good Book is insufficient for Christians who seek to obey God's Word and understand His will.

God has made promises to you, and He intends to keep them. So take God at His word: trust His promises and share them with your family, with your friends, and with the world.

We can have full confidence in God's promises because we can have full faith in His character.

Franklin Graham

There are four words I wish we would never forget, and they are, "God keeps his word."

Charles Swindoll

We have ample evidence that the Lord is able to guide. The promises cover every imaginable situation. All we need to do is to take the hand he stretches out.

Elisabeth Elliot

The stars may fall, but God's promises will stand and be fulfilled.

J. I. Packer

A HEALTHY THOUGHT FOR GARDENERS

By trusting in Thee, we know our labors are not in vain and that our harvest is great.

Jim G. Brown

A GARDENER'S PRAYER

Lord, Your Holy Word contains promises, and I will trust them. I will use the Bible as my guide, and I will trust You, Lord, to speak to me through Your Holy Spirit and through Your Holy Word, this day and forever. Amen

Too Busy?

Careful planning puts you ahead in the long run; hurry and scurry puts you further behind.

Proverbs 21:5 MSG

Has the hectic pace of life robbed you of the peace that might otherwise be yours through Jesus Christ? Are you one of those people who is simply too busy for your own good? If so, you're doing a disservice to yourself and your family.

Through His Son Jesus, God offers you a peace that passes human understanding, but He won't force His peace upon you; in order to experience it, you must slow down long enough to sense His presence and His love.

Today, as a gift to yourself, to your family, and to the world, be still and claim the inner peace that is your spiritual birthright—the peace of Jesus Christ. It is offered freely; it has been paid for in full; it is yours for the asking. So ask. And then share.

Often our lives are strangled by things that don't ultimately matter.

Grady Nutt

In our tense, uptight society where folks are rushing to make appointments they have already missed, a good laugh can be as refreshing as a cup of cold water in the desert.

Barbara Johnson

Being busy, in and of itself, is not a sin. But being busy in an endless pursuit of things that leave us empty and hollow and broken inside—that cannot be pleasing to God.

Max Lucado

We often become mentally and spiritually barren because we're so busy.

Franklin Graham

A HEALTHY THOUGHT FOR GARDENERS

You're only here for a short visit. Don't hurry, don't worry, and stop to smell the flowers along the way.

Walter Hagen

A GARDENER'S PRAYER

Dear Lord, when the quickening pace of life leaves me with little time for worship or for praise, help me to reorder my priorities, and let me turn to Jesus for the peace that only He can give. Amen

Giving Thanks for Christ's Love

Your old life is dead. Your new life, which is your real life—even though invisible to spectators—is with Christ in God. He is your life.

Colossians 3:3 MSG

Christ's love is perfect and steadfast. Even though we are fallible, and wayward, the Good Shepherd cares for us still. What does the love of Christ mean to His believers? It changes everything. Even though we have fallen far short of the Father's commandments, Christ loves us with a power and depth that is beyond our understanding. And, as we accept Christ's love and walk in Christ's footsteps, our lives bear testimony to His power and to His grace. Yes, Christ's love changes everything; may we invite Him into our hearts so it can then change everything in us.

Live your lives in love, the same sort of love which Christ gives us, and which He perfectly expressed when He gave Himself as a sacrifice to God.

Corrie ten Boom

So Jesus came, stripping himself of everything as he came—omnipotence, omniscience, omnipresence—everything except love. "He emptied himself" (Philippians 2:7), emptied himself of everything except love. Love—his only protection, his only weapon, his only method.

E. Stanley Jones

Jesus is all compassion. He never betrays us.

Catherine Marshall

No man ever loved like Jesus. He taught the blind to see and the dumb to speak. He died on the cross to save us. He bore our sins. And now God says, "Because He did, I can forgive you."

Billy Graham

A HEALTHY THOUGHT FOR GARDENERS

Cultivate the garden within.

Old Saying

A GARDENER'S PRAYER

Dear Jesus, my life has been changed forever by Your love and sacrifice. Today I will praise You, I will honor You, and I will walk with You. Amen

The Self-fulfilling Prophecy

May He grant you according to your heart's desire, and fulfill all your purpose.

Psalm 20:4 NKJV

The self-fulfilling prophecy is alive, well, and living at your house. If you trust God and have faith in the future, your optimistic beliefs will give you direction and motivation. That's one reason that you should never lose hope, but certainly not the only reason. The primary reason that you, as a believer, should never lose hope, is because of God's unfailing promises.

Make no mistake about it: thoughts are powerful things: your thoughts have the power to lift you up or to hold you down. When you acquire the habit of hopeful thinking, you will have acquired a powerful tool for improving your life. So if you fall into the habit of negative thinking, think again. After all, God's Word teaches us that Christ can overcome every difficulty (John 16:33). And when God makes a promise, He keeps it.

Our hope in Christ for the future is the mainstream of our joy.

C. H. Spurgeon

Oh, remember this: There is never a time when we may not hope in God. Whatever our necessities, however great our difficulties, and though to all appearance help is impossible, yet our business is to hope in God, and it will be found that it is not in vain.

George Mueller

I wish I could make it all new again; I can't. But God can. "He restores my soul," wrote the shepherd. God doesn't reform; he restores. He doesn't camouflage the old; he restores the new. The Master Builder will pull out the original plan and restore it. He will restore the vigor, he will restore the energy. He will restore the hope. He will restore the soul.

Max Lucado

A TIP FROM THE GARDEN

The two keys to success in gardening are understanding how plants grow and understanding how to provide them with a better home.

Sheryl London

A GARDENER'S PRAYER

Dear Lord, make me a hope-filled Christian. If I become discouraged, let me turn to You. If I grow weary, let me seek strength in You. In every aspect of my life, I will trust You, Father, today and forever. Amen

Discovering God's Plans

It is God who is at work in you, both to will and to work for His good pleasure.

Philippians 2:13 NASB

A righteous life doesn't happen by accident; like a bountiful garden, it must be cultivated with care.

If you seek to live in accordance with God's will for your life—and you should—then you will live in accordance with His commandments. You will study God's Word, and you will be watchful for His signs. You will associate with fellow Christians who will encourage your spiritual growth, and you will listen to that inner voice that speaks to you in the quiet moments of your daily devotionals.

God intends to use you in wonderful, unexpected ways if you let Him. The decision to seek God's plan and to follow it is yours and yours alone. The consequences of that decision have implications that are both profound and eternal, so choose carefully.

God has a plan for the life of every Christian. Every circumstance, every turn of destiny, all things work together for your good and for His glory.

Billy Graham

If not a sparrow falls upon the ground without your Father, you have reason to see that the smallest events of your career and your life are arranged by him.

C. H. Spurgeon

Every man's life is a plan of God.

Horace Bushnell

God is preparing you as his chosen arrow. As yet your shaft is hidden in his quiver, in the shadows, but, at the precise moment, he will reach for you and launch you to that place of his appointment.

Charles Swindoll

A TIP FROM THE GARDEN

Beauty is God's handwriting. Welcome it in every fair face, every fair sky, every fair flower.

Charles Kingsley

A GARDENER'S PRAYER

Dear Lord, You created me for a reason. Give me the wisdom to follow Your direction for my life's journey. Let me do Your work here on earth by seeking Your will and living it, knowing that when I trust in You, Father, I am eternally blessed. Amen

The Greatest of These

But now abide faith, hope, love, these three; but the greatest of these is love.

1 Corinthians 13:13 NASB

Love, like young seedlings in a garden, must be cultivated with care. And love, like every other thing in our universe, begins with God.

God's love for you is deeper and more profound than you can fathom. And now, precisely because you are a wondrous creation treasured by God, a question presents itself: What will you do in response to God's love? Will you ignore it or embrace it? Will you return it or neglect it? The decision, of course, is yours and yours alone.

When you embrace God's love, you are forever changed. When you embrace God's love, you feel differently about yourself, your family, your friends, and your world. When you embrace God's love, you share His message and you obey His commandments.

When you accept the Father's grace and share His love, you are blessed here on earth and throughout all eternity. Accept His love today . . . and share it always.

The cross symbolizes a cosmic as well as a historic truth. Love conquers the world, but its victory is not an easy one.

Reinhold Neibuhr

You can be sure you are abiding in Christ if you are able to have a Christlike love toward the people that irritate you the most.

Vonette Bright

Suppose that I understand the Bible. And, suppose that I am the greatest preacher who ever lived! The Apostle Paul wrote that unless I have love, "I am nothing."

Billy Graham

Christian love, either towards God or towards man, is an affair of the will.

C. S. Lewis

A HEALTHY THOUGHT FOR GARDENERS

The year's at the spring and day's at the morn; Morning's at seven; The hillside's dew-pearled; The lark's on the wing; The snail's on the thorn; God's in His heaven—All's right with the world.

Robert Browning

A GARDENER'S PRAYER

Lord, love is Your commandment. Help me always to remember that the gift of love is a precious gift indeed. Let me nurture love and treasure it, today and forever. Amen

Seeking God and Finding Happiness

But happy are those . . . whose hope is in the LORD their God.

Psalm 146:5 NLT

D o you sincerely want to be a happy Christian? Then set your mind and your heart upon God's love and His grace.

Happiness depends less upon our circumstances than upon our thoughts. When we turn our thoughts to God, to His gifts, and to His glorious creation, we experience the joy that God intends for His children. But, when we focus on the negative aspects of life, we suffer needlessly.

The fullness of life in Christ is available to all who seek it and claim it. Count yourself among that number. Seek first the salvation that is available through a personal relationship with Jesus Christ, and then claim the joy, the peace, and the spiritual abundance that the Shepherd offers His sheep.

Christ is the secret, the source, the substance, the center, and the circumference of all true and lasting gladness.

Mrs. Charles E. Cowman

God has charged Himself with full responsibility for our eternal happiness and stands ready to take over the management of our lives the moment we turn in faith to Him.

A. W. Tozer

True happiness consists only in the enjoyment of God. His favor is life, and his loving-kindness is better than life.

Arthur W. Pink

Happiness is not to be found in things, only in the secret places of the soul.

St. Thérèse of Lisieux

A HEALTHY THOUGHT FOR GARDENERS

Man is happy in a garden because God has made him so and to live in a garden is the nearest he can reach to paradise on earth.

Nan Fairbrother

A GARDENER'S PRAYER

Dear Lord, I am thankful for all the blessings You have given me. Let me be a happy Christian, Father, as I share Your joy with friends, with family, and with the world. Amen

Infinite Possibilities

Is anything too hard for the LORD?

Genesis 18:14 KJV

Are you afraid to ask God to do big things in your life? Is your faith threadbare and worn? If so, it's time to abandon your doubts and reclaim your faith in God's promises.

Ours is a God of infinite possibilities. But sometimes, because of limited faith and limited understanding, we wrongly assume that God cannot or will not intervene in the affairs of mankind. Such assumptions are simply wrong.

God's Holy Word makes it clear: absolutely nothing is impossible for the Lord. And since the Bible means what it says, you can be comforted in the knowledge that the Creator of the universe can do miraculous things in your own life and in the lives of your loved ones. Your challenge, as a believer, is to take God at His word, and to expect the miraculous.

If we take God's program, we can have God's power—not otherwise.

E. Stanley Jones

You can believe in the Holy Spirit not because you see Him, but because you see what He does in people's lives when they are surrendered to Christ and possess His power.

Billy Graham

The most profane word we use is "hopeless." When you say a situation or person is hopeless, you are slamming the door in the face of God.

Kathy Troccoli

There is Someone who makes possible what seems completely impossible.

Catherine Marshall

A HEALTHY THOUGHT FOR GARDENERS

The word "miracle" aptly describes a seed.

Jack Kramer

A GARDENER'S PRAYER

Dear God, in the garden I bear witness to Your miracles. I know that nothing is impossible for You—keep me always mindful of Your strength. When I lose hope, give me faith; when others lose hope, let me tell them of Your glory and Your works. Today, Lord, let me expect the miraculous, and let me trust in You. Amen

Enthusiasm for Today's Tasks

Whatever you do, work at it with all your heart, as working for the Lord, not for men.

Colossians 3:23 NIV

The gardener's life should be cause for celebration, but sometimes we don't feel much like celebrating. In fact, when the weight of the world seems to bear down upon our shoulders, celebration may be the last thing on our minds . . . but it shouldn't be. As God's children, we are all blessed beyond measure on good days and bad. This day is a non-renewable resource—once it's gone, it's gone forever. We should give thanks for this day while using it for the glory of God.

What will your attitude be today? Will you be fearful, angry, bored, or worried? Will you be cynical, bitter, or pessimistic? If so, God wants to have a little talk with you.

God created you in His own image, and He wants you to experience joy and abundance. But, God will not force His joy upon you; you must claim it for yourself. So today, and every day hereafter, celebrate the life that God has given you. Think optimistically about yourself and your future. Give thanks to the One who has given you everything, and trust in your heart that He wants to give you so much more.

Prayer must be aflame. Prayer without fervor is as a sun without light or heat, or as a flower without beauty or fragrance. A soul devoted to God is a fervent soul, and prayer is the creature of that flame. He only can truly pray who is all aglow for holiness, for God, and for heaven.

E. M. Bounds

Your enthusiasm will be infectious, stimulating, and attractive to others. They will love you for it. They will go for you and with you.

Norman Vincent Peale

Catch on fire with enthusiasm and people will come for miles to watch you burn.

John Wesley

A HEALTHY THOUGHT FOR GARDENERS

What I enjoy is not the fruits alone, but I also enjoy the soil itself.

Cicero

A GARDENER'S PRAYER

Dear Lord, I know that others are watching the way that I live my life. Help me to be an enthusiastic Christian with a faith that is contagious. Amen.

The Seeds of Forgiveness

Be kind to one another, tender-hearted, forgiving each other, just as God in Christ also has forgiven you.

Ephesians 4:32 NASB

Until we plant the seeds of forgiveness in our hearts, we will never reap the kind of bountiful harvest that God intends. Until we learn how to forgive, genuine love remains elusive. Why? Because even our most beloved friends and family members are imperfect (as are we). They need to be forgiven, and we need the experience of forgiving them (but not necessarily in that order).

Finding the generosity to forgive others is seldom easy, but if we truly desire to obey God's Word, we must learn to forgive our loved ones, just as we wish to be forgiven by them. Until we learn the art of forgiveness, we remain trapped in prisons of our own resentment and regret.

If, in your heart, you hold bitterness against even a single person, forgive. If there exists even one person, alive or dead, whom you have not forgiven, follow God's commandment and His will for your life: forgive. If you are embittered against yourself for some past mistake or shortcoming, forgive. Then, to the best of your abilities, forget. And move on. Bitterness and regret are not part of God's plan for your life. Forgiveness is.

Life is short, and we have not too much time for gardening the hearts of those who are traveling the dark way with us. Oh, be swift to love! Make haste to be kind.

Henri Frédéric Amiel

Forgiveness is actually the best revenge because it not only sets us free from the person we forgive, but it frees us to move into all that God has in store for us.

Stormie Omartian

Christians think they are prosecuting attorneys or judges, when, in reality, God has called all of us to be witnesses.

Warren Wiersbe

A HEALTHY THOUGHT FOR GARDENERS

Friendship is the garden of God; what a delight to tend his planting!

Inez Bell Ley

A GARDENER'S PRAYER

Dear Lord, sometimes forgiveness is difficult indeed. Today, Father, I ask You to help me move beyond feelings of bitterness and anger. Jesus forgave those who hurt Him; let me walk in His footsteps by forgiving those who have injured me. Amen

God's Guidebook

You will be a good servant of Christ Jesus, constantly nourished on the words of the faith and of the sound doctrine which you have been following.

1 Timothy 4:6 NASB

God has given us a guidebook for righteous living called the Holy Bible. It contains thorough instructions which, if followed, lead to fulfillment, righteousness, and salvation. But, if we choose to ignore God's commandments, the results are as predictable as they are tragic.

God has given us the Bible for the purpose of knowing His promises, His power, His commandments, His wisdom, His love, and His Son. As we study God's teachings and apply them to our lives, we live by the Word that shall never pass away.

Today, let us follow God's commandments, and let us conduct our lives in such a way that we might be shining examples to our students, to our families, and, most importantly, to those who have not yet found Christ.

The Bible is not a guidebook to a theological museum. It is a road map showing us the way into neglected or even forgotten glories of the living God.

Raymond Ortlund

The Bible is a Christian's guidebook, and I believe the knowledge it sheds on pain and suffering is the great antidote to fear for suffering people. Knowledge can dissolve fear as light destroys darkness.

Philip Yancey

The balance of affirmation and discipline, freedom and restraint, encouragement and warning is different for each child and season and generation, yet the absolutes of God's Word are necessary and trustworthy no matter how mercuric the time.

Gloria Gaither

A HEALTHY THOUGHT FOR GARDENERS

Kiss of the sun for pardon. / Song of the birds for mirth. / You're closer to God's heart in a garden, / than any place else on earth.

Dorothy Frances Gurney

A GARDENER'S PRAYER

Lord, You've given me instructions for life here on earth and for life eternal. I will use the Bible as my guide. I will study it and meditate upon it as I trust You, Lord, to speak to me through Your Holy Word. Amen

Giving Thanks to the Creator

In everything give thanks; for this is the will of God in Christ Jesus for you.

1 Thessalonians 5:18 NKJV

Every visit to the garden should be a cause for thanksgiving. Most of us have been blessed beyond measure, but sometimes, as busy people living in a demanding world, we are sometimes slow to count our gifts and even slower to give thanks to the Giver. Our blessings include life and health, family and friends, freedom and possessions—for starters. And those blessings are multiplied when we share them with others.

As the old saying goes, "When we drink the water, we should remember the spring." May we, who have been so richly blessed, give thanks for our gifts—and may we demonstrate our gratitude by sharing them.

God is worthy of our praise and is pleased when we come before Him with thanksgiving.

Shirley Dobson

The act of thanksgiving is a demonstration of the fact that you are going to trust and believe God.

Kay Arthur

Jesus wants Life for us, Life with a capital L.

John Eldredge

Where is God? He's right here at your side, my friend. He never left.

Charles Swindoll

A HEALTHY THOUGHT FOR GARDENERS

We are thankful to Thee for sunshine and rain and also for health and strength to enable us to work with Nature "from dawn to the setting sun."

Jim G. Brown

A GARDENER'S PRAYER

Dear Lord, help me have an attitude that is pleasing to You as I count my blessings today, tomorrow, and every day of my life. Whatever this day may hold—and whatever the harvest may be—let my response reflect a God-honoring attitude of optimism, faith, and love for You. Amen

DAY 29

The Simple Life

Whoever becomes simple and elemental again, like this child, will rank high in God's kingdom.

You live in a world where simplicity is in short supply. Think for a moment about the complexity of your everyday life and compare it to the lives of your ancestors. Certainly, you are the beneficiary of many technological innovations, but those innovations have a price: in all likelihood, your world is highly complex.

Unless you take firm control of your time and your life, you may be overwhelmed by an ever-increasing tidal wave of complexity that threatens your happiness. But your Heavenly Father understands the joy of living simply, and so should you. So do yourself a favor: keep your life as simple as possible. Simplicity is, indeed, genius. By simplifying your life, you are destined to improve it.

It is part of Satan's program to make our faith complicated and involved. Now and then, we need a rediscovery of the simplicity that is in Christ and in our faith in Him.

Vance Havner

Prescription for a happier and healthier life: resolve to slow down your pace; learn to say no gracefully; resist the temptation to chase after more pleasure, more hobbies, and more social entanglements.

James Dobson

Simplicity reaches out after God; purity discovers and enjoys him.

Thomas à Kempis

The most powerful life is the most simple life. The most powerful life is the life that knows where it's going, that knows where the source of strength is; it is the life that stays free of clutter and happenstance and hurriedness.

Max Lucado

A HEALTHY THOUGHT FOR GARDENERS

Good gardening is very simple, really. You just have to think like a plant.

Barbara Damrosch

A GARDENER'S PRAYER

Lord, help me keep it simple. When I complicate my life, give me the wisdom to simplify. The world values complexity, Father, but You do not. Today, I will strive to keep my thoughts focused intently on Your Word, on Your love, and on Your Son. Amen

Relying upon Him

Therefore humble yourselves under the mighty hand of God, that He may exalt you at the proper time, casting all your anxiety on Him, because He cares for you.

1 Peter 5:6-7 NASB

D o the demands of this day threaten to overwhelm you? If so, you must rely not only upon your own resources but also upon the promises of your Father in heaven.

God is a never-ending source of support and courage for those of us who call upon Him. When we are weary, He gives us strength. When we see no hope, God reminds us of His promises. When we grieve, God wipes away our tears.

God will hold your hand and walk with you every day of your life if you let Him. So even if your circumstances are difficult, trust the Father. His love is eternal and His goodness endures forever.

The more you give your mental burdens to the Lord, the more exciting it becomes to see how God will handle things that are impossible for you to do anything about.

Charles Swindoll

Faith is not merely you holding on to God—it is God holding on to you.

E. Stanley Jones

When you have no helpers, see all your helpers in God. When you have many helpers, see God in all your helpers. When you have nothing but God, see all in God; when you have everything, see God in everything. Under all conditions, stay thy heart only on the Lord.

C. H. Spurgeon

God uses our most stumbling, faltering faith-steps as the open door to His doing for us "more than we ask or think."

Catherine Marshall

A HEALTHY THOUGHT FOR GARDENERS

I will lift up my eyes to the hills—From whence comes my help? My help comes from the Lord, Who made heaven and earth.

Psalm 121:1-2 NKJV

A GARDENER'S PRAYER

Heavenly Father, You never leave or forsake me. You are always with me, protecting me and encouraging me. Whatever this day may bring, I thank You for Your love and Your strength. Amen

We Belong to Him

Now return to the LORD your God, For He is gracious and compassionate, Slow to anger, abounding in lovingkindness.

Joel 2:13 NASB

In the garden, we sense God's presence and His love. And as God's children, we are called to return the Father's love.

Christ made it clear: our first and greatest commandment is that we love God with all our hearts. When we worship God with faith and assurance, when we place Him at the absolute center of our lives, we invite His love into our hearts. When we do so, we are blessed beyond measure and beyond words.

St. Augustine wrote, "I love you, Lord, not doubtingly, but with absolute certainty. Your Word beat upon my heart until I fell in love with you, and now the universe and everything in it tells me to love you." Let us pray that we, too, will turn our hearts to our Father and to His Son. When we do, we are blessed in this life and throughout all eternity.

As perfectionists we find it difficult, if not impossible, to believe that God could completely accept, love, and long to be with us in this unfinished state.

Susan Lenzkes

God knows all that is true about us and is a friend to the face we show and the face we hide. He does not love us less for our human weaknesses.

Sheila Walsh

God loves me as God loves all people, without qualification. To be in the image of God means that all of us are made for the purpose of knowing and loving God and one another and of being loved in turn, not literally in the same way God knows and loves, but in a way appropriate to human beings.

Roberta Bondi

A HEALTHY THOUGHT FOR GARDENERS

Gardening is an instrument of grace.

Mary Sarton

A GARDENER'S PRAYER

Thank You, Lord, for Your love. Your love is boundless, infinite, and eternal. Today, as I pause and reflect upon Your love for me, let me share that love with all those who cross my path. And, as an expression of my love for You, Father, let me share the saving message of Your Son with a world in desperate need of His hope, His peace, and His salvation. Amen

Real Repentance

I preached that they should repent and turn to God and prove their repentance by their deeds.

Acts 26:20 NIV

Who among us has sinned? All of us. But the good news is this: When we do ask God's forgiveness and turn our hearts to Him, He forgives us absolutely and completely.

Genuine repentance requires more than simply offering God apologies for our misdeeds. Real repentance may start with feelings of sorrow and remorse, but it ends only when we turn away from the sin that has heretofore distanced us from our Creator. In truth, we offer our most meaningful apologies to God, not with our words, but with our actions. As long as we are still engaged in sin, we may be "repenting," but we have not fully "repented." So, if there is an aspect of your life that is distancing you from your God, ask for His forgiveness, and—just as importantly—stop sinning. Now.

Repentance involves a radical change of heart and mind in which we agree with God's evaluation of our sin and then take specific action to align ourselves with His will.

Henry Blackaby

True repentance is admitting that what God says is true, and that because it is true, we change our minds about our sins and about the Savior.

Warren Wiersbe

Repentance becomes a way of life, a lifelong process of turning towards the Holy One, that happens one day at a time.

Trevor Hudson

Repentance is the first conscious movement of the soul away from sin and toward God.

Sam Jones

A HEALTHY THOUGHT FOR GARDENERS

Did you ever think how a bit of land displays the character of the owner?

Laura Ingalls Wilder

A GARDENER'S PRAYER

When I stray from Your commandments, Lord, I must not only confess my sins, I must also turn from them. When I fall short, help me to change. Forgive my sins, Dear Lord, and help me live according to Your plan for my life. Your plan is perfect, Father; I am not. Let me trust in You. Amen

The Lessons of Tough Times

I waited patiently for the LORD; he turned to me and heard my cry. He lifted me out of the slimy pit, out of the mud and mire; he set my feet on a rock and gave me a firm place to stand. He put a new song in my mouth, a hymn of praise to our God....

Psalm 40:1-3 NIV

Sometimes the harvest is bountiful and sometimes it's not. Everybody makes mistakes. Your job is to make them only once.

Have you experienced a recent setback? If so, look for the lesson that God is trying to teach you. Instead of complaining about life's sad state of affairs, learn what needs to be learned, change what needs to be changed, and move on. View failure as an opportunity to reassess God's will for your life. View life's inevitable disappointments as opportunities to learn more about yourself and your world. If you are wise enough to learn from your experiences, you continue to mature throughout every stage of life. And that's precisely what God intends for you to do.

A weed is no more than a flower in disguise.

James Russell Lowell

Father, take our mistakes and turn them into opportunities.

Max Lucado

God is able to take mistakes, when they are committed to Him, and make of them something for our good and for His glory.

Ruth Bell Graham

The seeds of failure, when they are properly sown and carefully tended, can yield a bountiful harvest of success.

Jim Gallery

A HEALTHY THOUGHT FOR GARDENERS

A gardener learns more in the mistakes than in the successes.

Barbara Dodge Borland

A GARDENER'S PRAYER

Lord, I know that I am imperfect and that I fail You in many ways. Thank You for Your forgiveness and for Your unconditional love. Show me the error of my ways, Lord, that I might confess my wrongdoing and correct my mistakes. And, let me grow each day in wisdom, in faith, and in my love for You. Amen

Your Traveling Companion

But thanks be to God, who gives us the victory through our Lord Jesus Christ. Therefore, my beloved brethren, be steadfast, immovable, always abounding in the work of the Lord, knowing that your labor is not in vain in the Lord.

1 Corinthians 15:57-58 NKJV

As you continue to seek God's purpose for your life, you will undoubtedly experience your fair share of disappointments, detours, false starts, and failures. When you do, don't become discouraged: God's not finished with you yet.

The old saying is as true today as it was when it was first spoken: "Life is a marathon, not a sprint." That's why wise travelers select a traveling companion who never tires and never falters. That partner, of course, is your Heavenly Father. So pray as if everything depended upon God, and work as if everything depended upon you. And trust God to do the rest.

By perseverance the snail reached the ark.

C. H. Spurgeon

As we find that it is not easy to persevere in this being "alone with God," we begin to realize that it is because we are not "wholly for God." God has a right to demand that He should have us completely for Himself.

Andrew Murray

Failure is one of life's most powerful teachers. How we handle our failures determines whether we're going to simply "get by" in life or "press on."

Beth Moore

If things are tough, remember that every flower that ever bloomed had to go through a whole lot of dirt to get there.

Barbara Johnson

A TIP FROM THE GARDEN

Basic to an integrated life is a dominant ideal. To plow a straight row one must keep his eye on the goal rather than the plow.

J. M. Price

A GARDENER'S PRAYER

Dear Lord, when I want to give up, help me remember how important it is to keep trying. And when I'm worried or upset, help me remember to talk my family and friends and to You. Amen

Honoring God

Honor GOD with everything you own; give him the first and the best. Your barns will burst, your wine vats will brim over.

Proverbs 3:9-10 MSG

At times, your life is probably hectic, demanding, and complicated. When the demands of life leave you rushing from place to place with scarcely a moment to spare, you may fail to pause and thank your Creator for the blessings He has bestowed upon you. But that's a big mistake.

Whom will you choose to honor today? If you honor God and place Him at the center of your life, every day is a cause for celebration. But if you fail to honor your Heavenly Father, you're asking for trouble, and lots of it. So honor God for who He is and for what He has done for you. And don't just honor Him on Sunday morning. Praise Him all day long, every day, for as long as you live . . . and then for all eternity.

Happiness is to be found only in the home where God is loved and honored, where each one loves, and helps, and cares for the others.

St. Theophane Venard

God shows unbridled delight when He sees people acting in ways that honor Him.

Bill Hybels

We honor God by asking for great things when they are a part of His promise. We dishonor Him and cheat ourselves when we ask for molehills where He has promised mountains.

Vance Havner

What lessons about honor did you learn from your childhood? Are you living what you learned today?

Dennis Swanberg

A HEALTHY THOUGHT FOR GARDENERS

Flowers may beckon us, but they speak toward heaven and God.

Henry Ward Beecher

A GARDENER'S PRAYER

I praise You, Lord, from the depths of my heart, and I give thanks for Your goodness, for Your mercy, and for Your Son. Let me honor You every day of my life through my words and my deeds. Let me honor You, Father, with all that I am. Amen

An Intensely Bright Future: Yours

With God's power working in us, God can do much, much more than anything we can ask or imagine.

Ephesians 3:20 NCV

It takes courage to dream big dreams. You will discover that courage when you do three things: accept the past, trust God to handle the future, and make the most of the time He has given you today.

Are you excited about the opportunities of today and thrilled by the possibilities of tomorrow? Do you confidently expect God to lead you to a place of abundance, peace, and joy? And, when your days on earth are over, do you expect to receive the priceless gift of eternal life? If you trust God's promises, and if you have welcomed God's Son into your heart, then you should believe that your future is intensely and eternally bright.

No dreams are too big for God—not even yours. So start living—and dreaming—accordingly.

You cannot out-dream God.

John Eldredge

The biggest human temptation is to settle for too little.

Thomas Merton

Set goals so big that unless God helps you, you will be a miserable failure.

Bill Bright

The future lies all before us. Shall it only be a slight advance upon what we usually do? Ought it not to be a bound, a leap forward to altitudes of endeavor and success undreamed of before?

Annie Armstrong

A HEALTHY THOUGHT FOR GARDENERS

Gardeners, I think, dream bigger dreams than emperors.

Mary Cantwell

A GARDENER'S PRAYER

Dear Lord, my hope is in You. Give me the courage to face the future with certainty, and give me the wisdom to follow in the footsteps of Your Son, today and forever. Amen.

Give Me Patience, Lord, Right Now!

We urge you, brethren, admonish the unruly, encourage the fainthearted, help the weak, be patient with everyone.

1 Thessalonians 5:14 NASB

St. Augustine observed, "Patience is the companion of wisdom." Spoken like a true gardener. The plants in our gardens grow at their own pace and will not be hurried by fretful humans. That's why the best gardeners are patient gardeners.

If you're overly anxious for flowers to bloom or seedlings to sprout, slow down and allow God to do His work. God instructs you to be patient in all things—that means being patient with people and with gardens. And that's as it should be. After all, think about how patient God has been with you.

Our challenge is to wait in faith for the day of God's favor and salvation.

Jim Cymbala

How do you wait upon the Lord? First you must learn to sit at His feet and take time to listen to His words.

Kay Arthur

As we wait on God, He helps us use the winds of adversity to soar above our problems. As the Bible says, "Those who wait on the LORD . . . shall mount up with wings like eagles."

Billy Graham

Two signposts of faith: "Slow Down" and "Wait Here."

Charles Stanley

A TIP FROM THE GARDEN

A garden is a grand teacher. It teaches patience and careful watchfulness; it teaches industry and thrift; above all it teaches entire trust.

Gertrude Jekyll

A GARDENER'S PRAYER

Dear Lord, give me the wisdom to be patient. When I'm in a hurry for the flowers to bloom, give me peace. When I am frustrated by the inevitable ups and downs of life, give me perspective. When I am angry, keep me mindful of Your presence. Let me trust Your plans, Lord—with patience and thanksgiving—today and always. Amen

The World's Best Friend

Greater love has no one than this, that he lay down his life for his friends.

John 15:13 NIV

Who's the best friend this world has ever had? Jesus, of course! When you invite Him into your heart, Jesus will be your friend, too . . . your friend forever.

Jesus has offered to share the gifts of everlasting life and everlasting love with the world . . . and with you. If you make mistakes, He'll still be your friend. If you behave badly, He'll still love you. If you feel sorry or sad, He can help you feel better.

Jesus wants you to have a happy, healthy life. He wants you to be generous and kind. He wants you to follow His example. And the rest is up to you. You can do it! And with a friend like Jesus, you will.

The dearest friend on earth is but a mere shadow compared with Jesus Christ.

Oswald Chambers

What a friend we have in Jesus, all our sins and griefs to bear! What a privilege to carry everything to God in prayer! O what peace we often forfeit, O what needless pain we bear, all because we do not carry everything to God in prayer.

Joseph M. Scriven

When we are in a situation where Jesus is all we have, we soon discover he is all we really need.

Gigi Graham Tchividjian

Jesus be mine forever, my God, my heaven, my all.

C. H. Spurgeon

A HEALTHY THOUGHT FOR GARDENERS

I am the true vine, and My Father is the vineyard keeper. Every branch in Me that does not produce fruit He removes, and He prunes every branch that produces fruit so that it will produce more fruit.

John 15:1-2 HCSB

A GARDENER'S PRAYER

Dear Jesus, You are my Savior and my protector. Give me the courage to trust You completely. Today, I will praise You, I will honor You, and I will live according to Your commandments. Amen

A Godly Leader

But a good leader plans to do good, and those good things make him a good leader.

Isaiah 32:8 NCV

Leadership skills, like gardens, should be cultivated with care. Our world needs Christian leaders who willingly honor God with their words and their deeds, but not necessarily in that order.

If you seek to be a godly leader, then you must begin by being a worthy example to your family, to your friends, to your church, and to your community. After all, your words of instruction will never ring true unless you yourself are willing to follow them.

Are you the kind of leader whom you would want to follow? If so, congratulations. But if the answer to that question is no, then it's time to improve your leadership skills, beginning with the words that you speak and the example that you set, but not necessarily in that order.

The goal of leadership is to empower the whole people of God to discern and to discharge the Lord's will.

Stanley Grenz

A true and safe leader is likely to be one who has not desire to lead, but is forced into a position of leadership by inward pressure of the Holy Spirit and the press of external situation.

A. W. Tozer

A good leader is not the person who does things right, but the one who finds the right things to do.

Anthony T. Padovano

The man who kneels before God will stand before men.

Leonard Ravenhill

A HEALTHY THOUGHT FOR GARDENERS

All gardens are a form of autobiography.

Robert Dash

A GARDENER'S PRAYER

Dear Lord, when I find myself in a position of leadership, let me seek Your will and obey Your commandments. Let me be a Christ-centered leader, and let me turn to You, Father, for guidance, for courage, for wisdom, and for love. Amen

The Wisdom of Moderation

Moderation is better than muscle, self-control better than political power.

Proverbs 16:32 MSG

Moderation and wisdom are traveling companions. If we are wise, we must learn to temper our appetites, our desires, and our impulses. When we do, we are blessed, in part, because God has created a world in which temperance is rewarded and intemperance is inevitably punished.

Would you like to improve your life? Then harness your appetites and restrain your impulses. Moderation is difficult, of course; it is especially difficult in a prosperous society such as ours. But the rewards of moderation are numerous and long-lasting. Claim those rewards today. No one can force you to moderate your appetites. The decision to live temperately (and wisely) is yours and yours alone. And so are the consequences.

Every moment of resistance to temptation is a victory.

Frederick William Faber

We are all created differently. We share a common need to balance the different parts of our lives.

Dr. Walt Larimore

Virtue—even attempted virtue—brings light; indulgence brings fog.

C. S. Lewis

The key to healthy eating is moderation and managing what you eat every day.

John Maxwell

A TIP FROM THE GARDEN

Your job as a gardener is to try to keep things running smoothly for the plants and animals that live in or visit your yard, whatever the weather decides to do.

Ruth Shaw Ernst

A GARDENER'S PRAYER

Dear Lord, give me the wisdom to be moderate and self-disciplined. Let me strive to do Your will here on earth, and as I do, let me find contentment and balance. Let me be a disciplined believer, Father, today and every day. Amen

Shouting the Good News

As you go, preach this message: "The kingdom of heaven is near."

The Good News of Jesus Christ should be shouted from the rooftops by believers the world over. But all too often, it is not. For a variety of reasons, many Christians keep their beliefs to themselves, and when they do, the world suffers because of their failure to speak up.

Paul offered a message to believers of every generation when he wrote, "God has not given us a spirit of timidity" (2 Timothy 1:7 NASB). Paul's meaning is clear: When sharing our testimonies, we must be courageous, forthright, and unashamed. As believers in Christ, we know how He has touched our hearts and changed our lives. Now is the time to share our personal testimonies with others.

The old familiar hymn begins, "What a friend we have in Jesus . . . ." No truer words were ever penned. Jesus is the sovereign Friend and ultimate Savior of mankind. Christ showed enduring love for His believers by willingly sacrificing His own life so that we might have eternal life. Let us love Him, praise Him, and share His message of salvation with our neighbors and with the world.

God is not saving the world; it is done. Our business is to get men and women to realize it.

Oswald Chambers

For every believer, the task, or mission, is to lead people to the truth of Jesus Christ.

Charles Stanley

Taking the gospel to people wherever they are—death row, the ghetto, or next door—is frontline evangelism, frontline love. It is our one hope for breaking down barriers and for restoring the sense of community, of caring for one another, that our decadent, impersonalized culture has sucked out of us.

Chuck Colson

A HEALTHY THOUGHT FOR GARDENERS

When I go into my garden with a spade, and dig a bed, I feel such an exhilaration and health that I discover that I have been defrauding myself all this time in letting others do for me what I should have done with my own hands.

Ralph Waldo Emerson

A GARDENER'S PRAYER

Lord, even if I never leave home, make me a missionary for You. Let me share the Good News of Your Son, and let me tell of Your love and of Your grace. Make me a faithful servant for You, Father, now and forever. Amen

He Is Here

Where can I go from your Spirit? Where can I flee from your presence? If I go up to the heavens, you are there; if I make my bed in the depths, you are there. If I rise on the wings of the dawn, if I settle on the far side of the sea, even there your hand will guide me, your right hand will hold me fast.

Psalm 139:7-10 NIV

If God is everywhere, why does He sometimes seem so far away? The answer to that question, of course, has nothing to do with God and everything to do with us.

When we begin each day on our knees, in praise and worship to Him, God often seems very near indeed. But, if we ignore God's presence or—worse yet—rebel against it altogether, the world in which we live becomes a spiritual wasteland.

Today, and every day hereafter, cultivate a sense of God's constant protection. Talk to Him, thank Him, and praise Him. He is the Giver of all things good. Wherever you are, whether you are happy or sad, victorious or vanquished, celebrate God's presence. And be comforted. For He is here.

If your heart has grown cold, it is because you have moved away from the fire of His presence.

Beth Moore

God walks with us. He scoops us up in His arms or simply sits with us in silent strength until we cannot avoid the awesome recognition that yes, even now, He is here.

Gloria Gaither

Certainly, God is with us in times of distress, and that is a comforting truth. But listen: Jesus wants to be part of every experience and every moment of our lives.

Billy Graham

We may ignore, but we can nowhere evade, the presence of God. The world is crowded with Him. He walks everywhere incognito. And the incognito is not always hard to penetrate. The real labour is to remember, to attend. In fact, to come awake. Still more, to remain awake.

C. S. Lewis

A TIP FROM THE GARDEN

Flowers are sunshine, food, and medicine to the soul.

Luther Burbank

A GARDENER'S PRAYER

Heavenly Father, even when it seems to me that You are far away, You never leave my side. Today and every day, I will strive to feel Your presence, and I will strive to sense Your love for me. Amen

Conquering Everyday Frustrations

A hot-tempered man stirs up dissention, but a patient man calms a quarrel.

Proverbs 15:18 NIV

Life is full of frustrations: some great and some small. On occasion, you, like Jesus, will confront evil, and when you do, you may respond as He did: vigorously and without reservation. But, more often your frustrations will be of the more mundane variety. As long as you live here on earth, you will face countless opportunities to lose your temper over small, relatively insignificant events: a traffic jam, a spilled cup of coffee, an inconsiderate comment, a broken promise. When you are tempted to lose your temper over the minor inconveniences of life, don't. Turn away from anger, hatred, bitterness, and regret. Turn instead to God. When you do, you'll be following His commandments and giving yourself a priceless gift . . . the gift of peace.

Frustration is not the will of God. There is time to do anything and everything that God wants us to do.

Elisabeth Elliot

Anger is the noise of the soul; the unseen irritant of the heart; the relentless invader of silence.

Max Lucado

We must lay our questions, frustrations, anxieties, and impotence at the feet of God and wait for His answer. And then receiving it, we must live by faith.

Kay Arthur

Take no action in a furious passion. It's putting to sea in a storm.

Thomas Fuller

A HEALTHY THOUGHT FOR GARDENERS

My good hoe as it bites the ground revenges my wrongs, and I have less desire to bite my enemies. In smoothing the rough hillocks, I smooth my temper.

Ralph Waldo Emerson

A GARDENER'S PRAYER

Dear Lord, when I am angry, I cannot feel the peace that You intend for my life. When I am bitter, I cannot sense Your love. Heavenly Father, keep me mindful that forgiveness is Your commandment and Your will for my life. Let me turn away from anger and instead claim the spiritual abundance that You offer through the priceless gift of Your Son Jesus. Amen

Growing in Christ

When I was a child, I spoke as a child, I understood as a child, I thought as a child; but when I became a man, I put away childish things.

1 Corinthians 13:11 NKJV

Norman Vincent Peale had the following advice for believers of all ages: "Ask the God who made you to keep remaking you." That advice, of course, is perfectly sound, but often ignored.

The journey toward spiritual maturity lasts a lifetime. As Christians, we can and should continue to grow in the love and the knowledge of our Savior as long as we live.

When we cease to grow, either emotionally or spiritually, we do ourselves a profound disservice. But, if we study God's Word, if we obey His commandments, and if we live in the center of His will, we will not be "stagnant" believers; we will, instead, be growing Christians . . . and that's exactly what God wants for our lives.

With God, it isn't who you were that matters; it's who you are becoming.

Liz Curtis Higgs

Every great company, every great brand, and every great career has been built in exactly the same way: bit by bit, step by step, little by little.

John Maxwell

The instrument of our sanctification is the Word of God. The Spirit of God brings to our minds the precepts and doctrines of truth, and applies them with power. The truth is our sanctifier. If we do not hear or read it, we will not grow in sanctification.

C. H. Spurgeon

The process of growing up is to me valued for what we gain, not for what we lose.

C. S. Lewis

A HEALTHY THOUGHT FOR GARDENERS

Eventually, a gardener becomes a philosopher.

Barbara Dodge Borland

A GARDENER'S PRAYER

Dear Lord, I know that I still have so many things to learn. I won't stop learning, I won't give up, and I won't stop growing. Every day, I will do my best to become a little bit more like the person You intend for me to be. Amen

Time Is a Gift

So teach us to number our days, that we may gain a heart of wisdom.

Psalm 90:12 NKJV

The third chapter of Ecclesiastes reminds us that, "To every thing there is a season, and a time to every purpose under the heaven" (3:1 KJV). These words apply to all of life's endeavors, including gardening. In the garden, each passing season has its own special beauty and its own special purpose.

The message of every garden is the same: Sow, reap, and share—while there is still time.

Every day, like every life, is composed of moments. Each moment of your life holds within it the potential to seek God's will and to serve His purposes. If you are wise, you will strive to do both.

How will you invest the time that God has given you? Will you savor the moments of your life, or will you squander them? Will you use your time as an instrument of God's will, or will you allow commonplace distractions to rule your day and your life?

The gift of time is a gift from God. Treat it as if it were a precious, fleeting, one-of-a-kind treasure. Because it is.

Our time is short! The time we can invest for God, in creative things, in receiving our fellowmen for Christ, is short!

Billy Graham

To know and be known by Nature requires nothing more and nothing less than spending time with her as we would a cherished friend—listening, looking, revealing, laughing, crying, and praying together.

F. Lynne Bachleda

Our leisure, even our play, is a matter of serious concern. There is no neutral ground in the universe: every square inch, every split second, is claimed by God and counterclaimed by Satan.

C. S. Lewis

A HEALTHY THOUGHT FOR GARDENERS

All of us tend to put off living. We are all dreaming of some magical rose garden over the horizon instead of enjoying the roses that are blooming outside our windows today.

Dale Carnegie

A GARDENER'S PRAYER

Dear Lord, You have given me a wonderful gift: time here on earth. Let me use it wisely—for the glory of Your kingdom and the betterment of Your world. Amen

Experiencing Silence

Be still, and know that I am God.

Psalm 46:10 NKJV

O ne of the most important crops from any garden can—and should—be the feeling of peace that grows in the gardener's heart. That sense of peace is most readily achieved in silence.

The world seems to grow louder day by day, and our senses seem to be invaded at every turn. If we allow the distractions of a clamorous society to separate us from God's peace, we do ourselves a profound disservice. Our task, as dutiful believers, is to carve out moments of silence in a world filled with noise.

If we are to maintain righteous minds and compassionate hearts, we must take time each day for prayer and for meditation. We must make ourselves still in the presence of our Creator. We must quiet our minds and our hearts so that we might sense God's will and His love.

Has the busy pace of life robbed you of the peace that God has promised? If so, it's time to reorder your priorities and your life. Nothing is more important than the time you spend with your Heavenly Father. So be still and claim the inner peace that is found in the silent moments you spend with God.

It is in that stillness that the Voice will be heard, the only voice in all the universe that speaks peace to the deepest part of us.

Elisabeth Elliot

God is the friend of silence. Trees, flowers, grass grow in silence. See the stars, moon, and sun, how they move in silence.

Mother Teresa

The silence of nature is very real. It surrounds you. You can feel it.

Ted Trueblood

Quiet places should be enjoyed. Save the quiet places first.

Ernest Lyons

A HEALTHY THOUGHT FOR GARDENERS

In quietness and confidence shall be your strength.

Isaiah 30:15 NKJV

A GARDENER'S PRAYER

Dear Lord, whether I'm tending Your good earth or tending my own heart, help me remember the importance of silence. Help me discover quiet moments throughout the day so that I can sense Your presence and Your love. Amen

Richly Blessed

God loves a cheerful giver.

2 Corinthians 9:7 NIV

The words of Jesus are clear: "Freely you have received, freely give" (Matthew 10:8 NIV). As followers of Christ, we are commanded to be generous with our friends, with our families, and with those in need. We must give freely of our time, our possessions, and, most especially, our love.

In 2 Corinthians 9, Paul reminds us that when we sow the seeds of generosity, we reap bountiful rewards in accordance with God's plan for our lives. But Paul offers a word of caution: We are commanded to be cheerful givers—not to give "grudgingly or under compulsion" (v. 7).

Today, take God's words to heart and make this pledge: Be a cheerful, generous, courageous giver. The world needs your help, and you need the spiritual rewards that will be yours when you give it.

A happy spirit takes the grind out of giving. The grease of gusto frees the gears of generosity.

Charles Swindoll

If you want to be truly happy, you won't find it on an endless quest for more stuff. You'll find it in receiving God's generosity and in passing that generosity along.

Bill Hybels

The measure of a life, after all, is not its duration but its donation.

Corrie ten Boom

Let us give according to our incomes, lest God make our incomes match our gifts.

Peter Marshall

A HEALTHY THOUGHT FOR GARDENERS

As is the garden such is the gardener. A man's nature runs either to herbs or weeds.

Francis Bacon

A GARDENER'S PRAYER

Lord, You loved me before I was ever born; You sent Your Son Jesus to redeem me from my sins; You have given me the gift of eternal life. Today, I will share the priceless blessings that I have received: I will share my joy, my possessions, and my faith with others. Amen

Strength for Today

Those who hope in the LORD will renew their strength. They will soar on wings like eagles; they will run and not grow weary, they will walk and not be faint.

Isaiah 40:31 NIV

All of us have moments when we feel drained. All of us suffer through difficult days, trying times, and perplexing periods of our lives. Thankfully, God stands ready and willing to give us comfort and strength if we turn to Him.

Burning the candle at both ends is tempting but potentially destructive. Instead, we should place first things first by saying no to the things that we simply don't have the time or the energy to do. As we establish our priorities, we should turn to God and to His Holy Word for guidance.

If you're a person with too many demands and too few hours in which to meet them, don't fret. Instead, focus upon God and upon His love for you. Then, ask Him for the wisdom to prioritize your life and the strength to fulfill your responsibilities. God will give you the energy to do the most important things on today's to-do list . . . if you ask Him. So ask Him.

Worry does not empty tomorrow of its sorrow; it empties today of its strength.

Corrie ten Boom

When we reach the end of our strength, wisdom, and personal resources, we enter into the beginning of his glorious provisions.

Patsy Clairmont

In those desperate times when we feel like we don't have an ounce of strength, He will gently pick up our heads so that our eyes can behold something—something that will keep His hope alive in us.

Kathy Troccoli

A HEALTHY THOUGHT FOR GARDENERS

In my garden, care stops at the gate and gazes at me wistfully through the bars.

Alexander Smith

A GARDENER'S PRAYER

Lord, let me find my strength in You. When I am weary, give me rest. When I feel overwhelmed, let me look to You for my priorities. Let Your power be my power, Lord, and let Your way be my way, today and forever. Amen

Trust Your Conscience

So I strive always to keep my conscience clear before God and man.

Acts 24:16 NIV

Your conscience is an early-warning system designed to keep you out of trouble. When you're about to do something that you know is wrong, a little voice inside your head has a way of speaking up. If you listen to that voice, you'll be okay; if you ignore it, you're asking for headaches, or heartbreaks, or both.

Whenever you're about to make an important decision, you should listen carefully to the quiet voice inside. Sometimes, of course, it's tempting to do otherwise. From time to time you'll be tempted to abandon your better judgement by ignoring your conscience. But remember: a conscience is a terrible thing to waste. So instead of ignoring that quiet little voice, pay careful attention to it. If you do, your conscience will lead you in the right direction—in fact, it's trying to lead you right now. So listen . . . and learn.

Your conscience is your alarm system. It's your protection.

Charles Stanley

God desires that we become spiritually healthy enough through faith to have a conscience that rightly interprets the work of the Holy Spirit.

Beth Moore

You should not believe your conscience and your feelings more than the word which the Lord who receives sinners preaches to you.

Martin Luther

The beginning of backsliding means your conscience does not answer to the truth.

Oswald Sanders

A TIP FROM THE GARDEN

A modest garden contains, for those who know how to look and to wait, more instruction than a library.

Henri Frédéric Amiel

A GARDENER'S PRAYER

Dear God, You've given me a conscience that tells me right from wrong. Let me trust my conscience, and let me live according to Your teachings, not just for today, but forever. Amen

Encouraging Words for Family and Friends

Do not let any unwholesome talk come out of your mouths, but only what is helpful for building others up according to their needs, that it may benefit those who listen.

Ephesians 4:29 NIV

Life is a team sport, and all of us need occasional pats on the back from our teammates. As Christians, we are called upon to spread the Good News of Christ, and we are also called to spread a message of encouragement and hope to the world.

Whether you realize it or not, many people with whom you come in contact every day are in desperate need of a smile or an encouraging word. The world can be a difficult place, and countless friends and family members may be troubled by the challenges of everyday life. Since you don't always know who needs your help, the best strategy is to try to encourage all the people who cross your path. So today, be a world-class source of encouragement to everyone you meet. Never has the need been greater.

Encouragement is to a friendship what confetti is to a party.

Nicole Johnson

We do have the ability to encourage or discourage each other with the words we say. In order to maintain a positive mood, our hearts must be in good condition.

Annie Chapman

So often we think that to be encouragers we have to produce great words of wisdom when, in fact, a few simple syllables of sympathy and an arm around the shoulder can often provide much needed comfort.

Florence Littauer

A HEALTHY THOUGHT FOR GARDENERS

Man masters nature not by force but by understanding.

Jacob Bronowski

A GARDENER'S PRAYER

Dear Heavenly Father, because I am Your child, I am blessed. You have loved me eternally, cared for me faithfully, and saved me through the gift of Your Son Jesus. Just as You have lifted me up, Lord, let me lift up others in a spirit of encouragement and optimism and hope. And, if I can help a fellow traveler, even in a small way, Dear Lord, may the glory be Yours. Amen

God's Timetable

Humble yourselves, therefore, under God's mighty hand, that he may lift you up in due time.

1 Peter 5:6 NIV

Gardening is an exercise in patience. You simply can't hurry a plant because God's creations unfold according to His timetable, not our own.

Sometimes, the hardest thing to do is to wait. This is especially true when we're in a hurry and when we want things to happen now, if not sooner! But God's plan does not always happen in the way that we would like or at the time of our own choosing. Our task—as believing Christians who trust in a benevolent, all knowing Father—is to wait patiently for God to reveal Himself.

We human beings are, by nature, impatient. We know what we want, and we know exactly when we want it: RIGHT NOW! But, God knows better. He has created a world that unfolds according to His own timetable, not ours . . . thank goodness!

God is in no hurry. Compared to the works of mankind, He is extremely deliberate. God is not a slave to the human clock.

Charles Swindoll

Waiting on God brings us to the journey's end quicker than our feet.

Mrs. Charles E. Cowman

Will not the Lord's time be better than your time?

C. H. Spurgeon

God is not hurried along in the Time-stream of this universe any more than an author is hurried along in the imaginary time of his own novel. He has infinite attention to spare for each one of us. He does not have to deal with us in the mass. You are as much alone with Him as if you were the only being He had ever created. When Christ died, He died for you individually just as much as if you have been the only man in the world.

C. S. Lewis

A HEALTHY THOUGHT FOR GARDENERS

Many things grow in the garden that were never sown there.

Thomas Fuller

A GARDENER'S PRAYER

Dear Lord, Your timing is always right for me. You have a plan for my life that is grander than I can imagine. When I am impatient, remind me that You are never early or late. You are always on time, Father, so let me trust in You . . . always. Amen

Give Thanks for God's Word

Every word of God is flawless; he is a shield to those who take refuge in him.

Proverbs 30:5 NIV

God's Word is a roadmap for life here on earth and for life eternal. As Christians, we are called upon to study God's Holy Word, to trust its promises, to follow its commandments, and to share its Good News with the world.

As believers, we must study the Bible and meditate upon its meaning for our lives. Otherwise, we deprive ourselves of a priceless gift from our Creator. God's Holy Word is, indeed, a transforming, life-changing, one-of-a-kind treasure. And, a passing acquaintance with the Good Book is insufficient for Christians who seek to obey God's Word and to understand His will. After all, neither man nor woman should live by bread alone . . .

Walking in faith brings you to the Word of God. There you will be healed, cleansed, fed, nurtured, equipped, and matured.

Kay Arthur

God did not write a book and send it by messenger to be read at a distance by unaided minds. He spoke a Book and lives in His spoken words, constantly speaking His words and causing the power of them to persist across the years.

A. W. Tozer

The only way we can understand the Bible is by personal contact with the Living Word.

Oswald Chambers

There is no way to draw closer to God unless you are in the Word of God every day. It's your compass. Your guide. You can't get where you need to go without it.

Stormie Omartian

A HEALTHY THOUGHT FOR GARDENERS

On Saturday evening, when we listen to the radio and shell our dried beans, we are able to relax after our week's work and realize that there is more happiness in simple living than in glamour.

Jim G. Brown

A GARDENER'S PRAYER

Heavenly Father, Your Holy Word is a light unto my path. In all that I do, help me be a worthy witness for You as I share the Good News of Your perfect Son and Your perfect Word. Amen

Actions That Reflect Our Beliefs

If the way you live isn't consistent with what you believe, then it's wrong.

Romans 14:23 MSG

Are you the kind of practical Christian who is willing to dig in and do what needs to be done when it needs to be done? If so, congratulations: God acknowledges your service and blesses it. But if you find yourself more interested in the fine points of theology than in the needs of your neighbors, it's time to rearrange your priorities.

As Christians, we must do our best to ensure that our actions are accurate reflections of our beliefs. Our theology must be demonstrated, not only by our words but, more importantly, by our actions. In short, we should be practical believers, quick to act whenever we see an opportunity to serve God.

God needs believers who are willing to roll up their sleeves and go to work for Him. Count yourself among that number. Theology is a good thing unless it interferes with God's work. And it's up to you to make certain that your theology doesn't.

Do noble things, do not dream them all day long.

Charles Kingsley

Although our actions have nothing to do with gaining our own salvation, they might be used by God to save somebody else! What we do really matters, and it can affect the eternities of people we care about.

Bill Hybels

Let us not be content to wait and see what will happen, but give us the determination to make the right things happen.

Peter Marshall

It is by acts and not by ideas that people live.

Harry Emerson Fosdick

A HEALTHY THOUGHT FOR GARDENERS

Growing a garden and staying out in the fresh air after office hours seemed to give me the strength to meet all problems with greater courage.

Jim G. Brown

A GARDENER'S PRAYER

Heavenly Father, I believe in You, and I believe in Your Word. Help me to live in such a way that my actions validate my beliefs—and let the glory be Yours forever. Amen

The Right Kind of Behavior

By this we know that we have come to know Him, if we keep His commandments.

1 John 2:3 NASB

When we seek righteousness in our own lives—and when we seek the companionship of those who do likewise—we reap the spiritual rewards that God intends for us to enjoy. When we behave ourselves as godly men and women, we honor God. When we live righteously and according to God's commandments, He blesses us in ways that we cannot fully understand.

Today, as you fulfill your responsibilities, hold fast to that which is good, and associate yourself with believers who behave themselves in like fashion. When you do, your good works will serve as a powerful example for others and as a worthy offering to your Creator.

Christians are the citizens of heaven, and while we are on earth, we ought to behave like heaven's citizens.

Warren Wiersbe

Be such a man, and live such a life, that if every man were such as you, and every life a life like yours, this earth would be God's Paradise.

Phillips Brooks

We should live in light of being called out of this world at any time into the presence of God, where we will receive our eternal reward.

John MacArthur

A TIP FROM THE GARDEN

Listen to the sermon preached to you by the flowers, the trees, the shrubs, the sky, and the whole world. Notice how they preach to you a sermon full of love, of praise of God, and how they invite you to glorify the sublimity of that sovereign Artist who has given them being.

Paul of the Cross

A GARDENER'S PRAYER

Dear Lord, this world has countless temptations, distractions, interruptions, and frustrations. When I allow my focus to drift away from You and Your Word, I suffer. But, when I turn my thoughts and my prayers to You, Heavenly Father, You guide my path. Let me discover the right thing to do—and let me do it—this day and every day that I live. Amen

His Rule, Your Rule

Here is a simple, rule-of-thumb for behavior: Ask yourself what you want people to do for you, then grab the initiative and do it for them. Add up God's Law and Prophets and this is what you get.

Matthew 7:12 MSG

As Christians, we are instructed to be courteous and compassionate. As believers, we are called to be gracious, humble, gentle, and kind. But sometimes, we fall short. Sometimes, amid the busyness and confusion of everyday life, we may neglect to share a kind word or a kind deed. This oversight hurts others, and it hurts us as well.

Today, slow yourself down and be alert for those who need your smile, your kind words, or your helping hand. Make kindness a centerpiece of your dealings with others. They will be blessed, and you will be, too. So make this promise to yourself and keep it: Honor Christ by obeying His Golden Rule. He deserves no less.

It is wrong for anyone to be anxious to receive more from his neighbor than he himself is willing to give to God.

St. Francis of Assisi

To keep the Golden Rule we must put ourselves in other people's places, but to do that consists in and depends upon picturing ourselves in their places.

Harry Emerson Fosdick

It is my calling to treat every human being with grace and dignity, to treat every person, whether encountered in a palace or a gas station, as a life made in the image of God.

Sheila Walsh

It is one of the most beautiful compensations of life that no one can sincerely try to help another without helping herself.

Barbara Johnson

A TIP FROM THE GARDEN

Gardening has compensations out of all proportion to its goals. It is creation in the pure sense.

Phyllis McGinley

A GARDENER'S PRAYER

Lord, I thank You for friends and family members who practice the Golden Rule. Because I expect to be treated with kindness, let me be kind. Because I wish to be loved, let me be loving. In all things, Lord, let me live by the Golden Rule, and let me express my gratitude to those who offer kindness to me. Amen

Gratitude and Enthusiasm

So roll up your sleeves, put your mind in gear, be totally ready to receive the gift that's coming when Jesus arrives. Don't lazily slip back into those old grooves of evil, doing just what you feel like doing. You didn't know any better then; you do now. As obedient children, let yourselves be pulled into a way of life shaped by God's life, a life energetic and blazing with holiness.

1 Peter 1:13-15 MSG

Dietrich Bonhoeffer observed, "It is only with gratitude that life becomes rich." These words certainly apply to every gardener, including you. Are you a grateful gardener? Do you appreciate the gifts that God has given you? And, do you demonstrate your gratitude by being an enthusiastic steward of the gifts and talents that you have received from your Creator? You most certainly should be enthusiastic. After all, when you stop to think about it, God has given you more blessings than you can count.

God is always watching and listening. Are you an enthusiastic believer, and are you constantly thanking Him for His gifts? Hopefully so, because the best moment to demonstrate your gratitude is always the present moment.

We act as though comfort and luxury were the chief requirements of life, when all we need to make us really happy is something to be enthusiastic about.

Charles Kingsley

One of the great needs in the church today is for every Christian to become enthusiastic about his faith in Jesus Christ.

Billy Graham

Enthusiasm, like the flu, is contagious—we get it from one another.

Barbara Johnson

Diligence applies to whatever you do in your Christian life. Anything done in the Lord's service is worth doing with enthusiasm and care.

John MacArthur

A HEALTHY THOUGHT FOR GARDENERS

I look upon the pleasure which we take in a garden as one of the most innocent delights in human life.

Cicero

A GARDENER'S PRAYER

Dear Lord, let me be an enthusiastic participant in life. And let my enthusiasm bring honor and glory to You. Amen

Cultivating Hope

These things I have spoken to you, that in Me you may have peace. In the world you will have tribulation; but be of good cheer, I have overcome the world.

John 16:33 NKJV

Hope, like the plants in a garden, must be cultivated with care. If we leave our hopes untended—or if we contaminate them with the twin poisons of discouragement and doubt—the gardens of our souls produce few fruits. But, if we nurture our hopes through a firm faith in God and a realistic faith in ourselves, we bring forth bountiful harvests that bless us, our families, and generations yet unborn. It is best that we cultivate our hopes each day through quiet meditation, through devotion to God, and through association with encouraging family members and friends. But sometimes, amid the hustle and bustle of life here on earth, we leave our hopes to fend for themselves, and when we do, bad things begin to happen: Like weeds overtaking a flower garden, our worries can quickly overtake our thoughts. The only solution, of course, is to dig in, to pull the weeds, and to reclaim the flowers.

If the garden of your soul has been overtaken by the negativity that is an unfortunate hallmark of the age in which we live, don't be discouraged. Simply turn your thoughts and prayers to the Father and to the Son. Then trust in God's promises. And finally, make the resolution to tend your spiritual garden every day that you live. A garden is a lovely place to visit if it is tended with care, so cultivate yours carefully, and then reap the bountiful harvest that God has in store for you.

When you say a situation or a person is hopeless, you are slamming the door in the face of God.

Charles Allen

The Lord Himself has laid the foundation of His people's hopes. We must determine if our hopes are built on this foundation.

C. H. Spurgeon

A HEALTHY THOUGHT FOR GARDENERS
Where flowers bloom so does hope.

Lady Bird Johnson

A GARDENER'S PRAYER
Lord, let me be filled with hope whether I'm in my garden or not. Let me expect the best from You, and let me look for the best in others. Let me trust You, Lord, to direct every aspect of my life. And, let me be Your faithful, hopeful, optimistic servant every day that I live. Amen

You Are Blessed

I will bless them and the places surrounding my hill. I will send down showers in season; there will be showers of blessings.

Ezekiel 34:26 NIV

Your garden is a gift from God, one of many that He has bestowed. Have you counted your blessings lately? If you sincerely wish to follow in Christ's footsteps, you should make thanksgiving a habit, a regular part of your daily routine.

We honor God, in part, by the genuine gratitude we feel in our hearts for His blessings. Yet even the most saintly among us must endure periods of apathy, times when we are not fully aware of—or fully grateful for—the blessings and opportunities that God has entrusted to our care. Why? Because we are imperfect human beings who are incapable of perfect gratitude.

Even on life's darker days, we must make the effort to cleanse our hearts of negative emotions and fill them, instead, with praise, with love, with hope, and with thanksgiving. To do otherwise is to be unfair to ourselves, to our loved ones, and to our God.

When God blesses us, He expects us to use those blessings to bless the lives of others.

Jim Gallery

You cannot persevere unless there is a trial in your life. There can be no victories without battles; there can be no peaks without valleys. If you want the blessing, you must be prepared to carry the burden and fight the battle. God has to balance privileges with responsibilities, blessings with burdens, or else you and I will become spoiled, pampered children.

Warren Wiersbe

Think of the blessings we so easily take for granted: Life itself; preservation from danger; every bit of health we enjoy; every hour of liberty; the ability to see, to hear, to speak, to think, and to imagine all this comes from the hand of God.

Billy Graham

A TIP FROM THE GARDEN

There is something about sun and soil that heals broken bodies and jangled nerves.

Nature Magazine

A GARDENER'S PRAYER

Lord, I have more blessings than I can possibly count; make me mindful of Your precious gifts. You have cared for me, Lord, and You have saved me. I will give thanks and praise You always. Today, let me share Your blessings with others, just as You first shared them with me. Amen

Cheerfulness 101

A miserable heart means a miserable life; a cheerful heart fills the day with a song.

Proverbs 15:15 MSG

Christ promises us lives of abundance and joy, but He does not force His joy upon us. We must claim His joy for ourselves, and when we do, Jesus, in turn, fills our spirits with His power and His love. Few things in life are more sad, or, for that matter, more absurd, than a grumpy Christian.

How can we receive from Christ the joy that is rightfully ours? By giving Him what is rightfully His: our hearts and our souls.

When we earnestly commit ourselves to the Savior of mankind, when we place Jesus at the center of our lives and trust Him as our personal Savior, He will transform us, not just for today, but for all eternity. Then we, as God's children, can share Christ's joy and His message with a world that needs both.

Christ can put a spring in your step and a thrill in your heart. Optimism and cheerfulness are products of knowing Christ.

Billy Graham

It is not fitting, when one is in God's service, to have a gloomy face or a chilling look.

St. Francis of Assisi

When I think of God, my heart is so full of joy that the notes leap and dance as they leave my pen; and since God has given me a cheerful heart, I serve him with a cheerful spirit.

Franz Joseph Haydn

We may run, walk, stumble, drive, or fly, but let us never lose sight of the reason for the journey, or miss a chance to see a rainbow on the way.

Gloria Gaither

A TIP FROM THE GARDEN

Flowers are like human beings. They thrive on a little kindness.

Fred Streeter

A GARDENER'S PRAYER

Dear Lord, You have given me so many reasons to be happy, and I want to be a cheerful Christian. Today and every day, I will do my best to share my happiness with my family and my friends. Amen

Let God Decide

A man's heart plans his way, but the Lord directs his steps.

Proverbs 16:9 NKJV

The world will often lead you astray, but God will not. His counsel leads you to Himself, which, of course, is the path He has always intended for you to take. Are you facing a difficult decision, a troubling circumstance, or a powerful temptation? If so, it's time to step back, to stop focusing on the world, and to focus, instead, on the will of your Father in heaven.

Everyday living is an exercise in decision-making. Today and every day you must make choices: choices about what you will do, what you will worship, and how you will think. When in doubt, make choices that you sincerely believe will bring you to a closer relationship with God. And if you're uncertain of your next step, pray about it. When you do, answers will come—the right answers for you.

As we trust God to give us wisdom for today's decisions, He will lead us a step at a time into what He wants us to be doing in the future.

Theodore Epp

God always gives His best to those who leave the choice with Him.

Jim Elliot

There is no need to fear the decisions of life when you know Jesus Christ, for His name is Counselor.

Warren Wiersbe

I don't doubt that the Holy Spirit guides your decisions from within when you make them with the intention of pleasing God. The error would be to think that He speaks only within, whereas in reality He speaks also through Scripture, the Church, Christian friends, and books.

C. S. Lewis

A HEALTHY THOUGHT FOR GARDENERS

I have often thought that if heaven had given me choice of my position and calling, it should have been on a rich spot of earth, well watered, and near a good market for the productions of the garden.

Thomas Jefferson

A GARDENER'S PRAYER

Lord, help me to make decisions that are pleasing to You. Help me to be honest, patient, thoughtful, and obedient. And above all, help me to follow the teachings of Jesus, not just today, but every day. Amen

The Temptation to Judge

When they continued to ask Jesus their question, he raised up and said, "Anyone here who has never sinned can throw the first stone at her."

John 8:7 NCV

The warning of Matthew 7:1 is clear: "Judge not, that ye be not judged" (KJV). Yet even the most devoted Christians may fall prey to a powerful yet subtle temptation: the temptation to judge others. But as obedient followers of Christ, we are commanded to refrain from such behavior.

As Jesus came upon a young woman who had been condemned by the Pharisees, He spoke not only to the crowd that was gathered there, but also to all generations when He warned, "He that is without sin among you, let him first cast a stone at her" (John 8:7 KJV). Christ's message is clear, and it applies not only to the Pharisees of ancient times, but also to us.

Forget the faults of others by remembering your own.

John Bunyan

Only Christ can free us from the prison of legalism, and then only if we are willing to be freed.

Madeleine L'Engle

Judging draws the judgment of others.

Catherine Marshall

Being critical of others, including God, is one way we try to avoid facing and judging our own sins.

Warren Wiersbe

A TIP FROM THE GARDEN

Think about the garden as a small community of plants and animals coexisting with one another and with human beings.

Ruth Shaw Ernst

A GARDENER'S PRAYER

Dear Lord, sometimes I am quick to judge others. But, You have commanded me not to judge. Keep me mindful, Father, that when I judge others, I am living outside of Your will for my life. You have forgiven me, Lord. Let me forgive others, let me love them, and let me help them . . . without judging them. Amen

The World . . . and You

Don't copy the behavior and customs of this world, but let God transform you into a new person by changing the way you think.

Romans 12:2 NLT

We live in the world, but we must not worship it. Our duty is to place God first and everything else second. But because we are fallible beings with imperfect faith, placing God in His rightful place is often difficult. In fact, at every turn, or so it seems, we are tempted to do otherwise.

The 21st-century world is a noisy, distracting place filled with countless opportunities to stray from God's will. The world seems to cry, "Worship me with your time, your money, your energy, and your thoughts!" But God commands otherwise: He commands us to worship Him and Him alone; everything else must be secondary.

C. S. Lewis said, "Aim at heaven and you will get earth thrown in; aim at earth and you will get neither." That's good advice. You're likely to hit what you aim at, so aim high . . . aim at heaven. When you do, you'll be strengthening your character as you improve every aspect of your life. And God will demonstrate His approval as He showers you with more spiritual blessings than you can count.

Because the world is deceptive, it is dangerous. The world can even deceive God's own people and lead them into trouble.

Warren Wiersbe

Our fight is not against any physical enemy; it is against organizations and powers that are spiritual. We must struggle against sin all our lives, but we are assured we will win.

Corrie ten Boom

A fish would never be happy living on land, because it was made for water. An eagle could never feel satisfied if it wasn't allowed to fly. You will never feel completely satisfied on earth, because you were made for more.

Rick Warren

A HEALTHY THOUGHT FOR GARDENERS

How fair is a garden amid the toils and passions of existence.

Benjamin Disraeli

A GARDENER'S PRAYER

Dear Lord, I am an imperfect human being living in an imperfect world. Direct my path far from the temptations and distractions of this world, and let me follow in the footsteps of Your Son today and forever. Amen

Using God's Gifts

God has given gifts to each of you from his great variety of spiritual gifts. Manage them well so that God's generosity can flow through you.

1 Peter 4:10 NLT

God gives us talents for a reason: to use them. Each of us possesses special abilities, gifted by God, that can be nurtured carefully or ignored totally. Our challenge, of course, is to use our talents to the greatest extent possible. But we are mightily tempted to do otherwise. Why? Because converting raw talent into polished skill usually requires work, and lots of it. God's Word clearly instructs us to do the hard work of refining our talents for the glory of His kingdom and the service of His people.

The old saying is both familiar and true: "What we are is God's gift to us; what we become is our gift to God." May we always remember that our talents and abilities are priceless gifts from our Creator, and that the best way to say "thank you" for those gifts is to use them.

Today, make a promise to yourself that you will earnestly seek to discover the talents that God has given you. Then, cultivate those talents and make them grow. Finally, vow to share your gifts with the world for as long as God gives you the power to do so.

When God crowns our merits, he is crowning nothing other than his gifts.

St. Augustine

Almighty God created us, redeemed us, called us, endowed us with gifts and abilities and perceptions. To demean the gift is to insult the Giver.

Penelope Stokes

There's a unique sense of fulfillment that comes when we submit our gifts to God's use and ask him to energize them in a supernatural way—and then step back to watch what he does. It can be the difference between merely existing in black and white and living a life in full, brilliant color.

Lee Strobel

A HEALTHY THOUGHT FOR GARDENERS

The farmer who takes everything from the land without restitution will become the servant of wiser men, either on the farm or elsewhere.

C. E. Thorne

A GARDENER'S PRAYER

Dear Lord, let me use my gifts, and let me help others discover theirs. Your gifts are priceless and eternal. May we, Your children, use them to the glory of Your kingdom, today and forever. Amen

The Remedy for Uncertainty

He replied, "You of little faith, why are you so afraid?" Then he got up and rebuked the winds and the waves, and it was completely calm.

Matthew 8:26 NIV

Sometimes, like Jesus' disciples, we feel threatened by the storms of life. During these moments, when our hearts are flooded with uncertainty, we must remember that God is not simply near, He is here.

Have you ever felt your faith in God slipping away? If so, you are in good company. Even the most faithful Christians are, at times, beset by occasional bouts of discouragement and doubt. But even when you feel far removed from God, God never leaves your side. He is always with you, always willing to calm the storms of life. When you sincerely seek His presence—and when you genuinely seek to establish a deeper, more meaningful relationship with His Son—God will calm your fears, answer your prayers, and restore your soul.

We basically have two choices to make in dealing with the mysteries of God. We can wrestle with Him or we can rest in Him.

Calvin Miller

There is a difference between doubt and unbelief. Doubt is a matter of mind: we cannot understand what God is doing or why He is doing it. Unbelief is a matter of will: we refuse to believe God's Word and obey what He tells us to do.

Warren Wiersbe

Mark it down. God never turns away the honest seeker. Go to God with your questions. You may not find all the answers, but in finding God, you know the One who does.

Max Lucado

A HEALTHY THOUGHT FOR GARDENERS

Gardening is medicine that does not need a prescription.

Old Saying

A GARDENER'S PRAYER

Dear God, sometimes this world can be a puzzling place, filled with uncertainty and doubt. When I am unsure of my next step, keep me mindful that You are always near and that You can overcome any challenge. With Your love and Your power, Father, I can live courageously and faithfully, today and every day. Amen

Thanksgiving Yes...
Envy No!

Stop your anger! Turn from your rage! Do not envy others—it only leads to harm.

Psalm 37:8 NLT

As the recipient of God's grace, you have every reason to celebrate life. After all, God has promised you the opportunity to receive His abundance and His joy—in fact, you have the opportunity to receive those gifts right now. But if you allow envy to gnaw away at the fabric of your soul, you'll find that joy remains elusive. So do yourself an enormous favor: Rather than succumbing to the sin of envy, focus on the marvelous things that God has done for you—starting with Christ's sacrifice. Thank the Giver of all good gifts, and keep thanking Him for the wonders of His love and the miracles of His creation. Count your own blessings and let your neighbors count theirs. It's the godly way to live.

Too many Christians envy the sinners their pleasures and the saint their joy, because they don't have either one.

Martin Luther

How can you possess the miseries of envy when you possess in Christ the best of all portions?

C. H. Spurgeon

When you worry about what you don't have, you won't be able to enjoy what you do have.

Charles Swindoll

God is worthy of our praise and is pleased when we come before Him with thanksgiving.

Shirley Dobson

A HEALTHY THOUGHT FOR GARDENERS

Flowers and plants are silent presences; they nourish every sense but the ear.

Mary Sarton

A GARDENER'S PRAYER

Dear Lord, deliver me from the needless pain of envy. You have given me countless blessings. Let me be thankful for the gifts I have received, and let me never be resentful of the gifts You have given others. Amen

Walking in His Footsteps

I've laid down a pattern for you. What I've done, you do.

John 13:15 MSG

As citizens of a fast-changing world, we face challenges that sometimes leave us feeling overworked, over-committed, and overwhelmed. But God has different plans for us. He intends that we slow down long enough to praise Him and to glorify His Son.

Each day, we are confronted with countless opportunities to serve God and to follow in the footsteps of His Son. When we do, our Heavenly Father guides our steps and blesses our endeavors. He lifts our spirits and enriches our lives.

Today provides a glorious opportunity to place yourself in the service of the One who is the Giver of all blessings. May you seek His will, may you trust His word, and may you walk in the footsteps of His Son.

We have in Jesus Christ a perfect example of how to put God's truth into practice.

Bill Bright

Christ is to be sought and bought with any pains, at any price; we cannot buy this gold too dear. He is a jewel worth more than a thousand worlds. Get him, and get all; miss him and miss all.

Thomas Brooks

To walk out of His will is to walk into nowhere.

C. S. Lewis

Imagine the spiritual strength the disciples drew from walking hundreds of miles with Jesus . . . 3 John 4.

Jim Maxwell

A HEALTHY THOUGHT FOR GARDENERS

It is good to be alone in a garden at dawn or dark so that all its shy presences may haunt you and possess you in a reverie of suspended thought.

James Douglas

A GARDENER'S PRAYER

Dear Jesus, because I am Your disciple, I will trust You, I will obey Your teachings, and I will share Your Good News. You have given me life abundant and life eternal, and I will follow You today and forever. Amen

In His Hands

Don't brashly announce what you're going to do tomorrow; you don't know the first thing about tomorrow.

Proverbs 27:1 MSG

Every garden is a leap of faith. Every garden is a statement of trust in the future. Every garden is declaration of hope. We sow our seeds in the springtime, hoping to reap a harvest that is eagerly anticipated but, as of yet, unseen. And so it is with life. Each day, as we tend to the necessities of life, we plant seeds for the future. When we plant wisely and trust God completely, the harvest is bountiful.

When we trust God, we must trust Him without reservation. We must steel ourselves against the inevitable disappointments of the day, secure in the knowledge that our Heavenly Father has a plan for the future that we cannot see.

Can you place your future into the hands of a loving and all-knowing God? Can you live amid the uncertainties of today, knowing that God has dominion over all your tomorrows? If you can, you are wise and you are blessed. When you trust God with everything you are and everything you have, He will give you strength and life, not just for today, but for eternity.

That we may not complain of what is, let us see God's hand in all events; and, that we may not be afraid of what shall be, let us see all events in God's hand.

Matthew Henry

Hoping for a good future without investing in today is like a farmer waiting for a crop without ever planting any seed.

John Maxwell

Tomorrow's history has already been written—at the name of Jesus every knee must bow.

Paul E. Kauffman

A TIP FROM THE GARDEN

One of the most delightful things about a garden is the anticipation it provides.

W. E. Johns

A GARDENER'S PRAYER

Dear Lord, as I look to the future, I will place my trust in You. If I become discouraged, I will turn to You. If I am weak, I will seek strength in You. You are my Father, and I will place my hope, my trust, and my faith in You. Amen

Cultivating Wisdom

He who walks with the wise grows wise . . . .

Proverbs 13:20 NIV

Wisdom does not spring up overnight—it takes time. To become wise, we must seek God's wisdom and live according to His Word. And, we must not only learn the lessons of the Christian life, we must also live by them.

Do you seek to live a life of righteousness and wisdom? If so, you must study the ultimate source of wisdom: the Word of God. You must seek out worthy mentors and listen carefully to their advice. You must associate, day in and day out, with godly men and women. And, you must act in accordance with your beliefs. When you do these things, you will become wise . . . and you will be a blessing to your friends, to your family, and to the world.

When you and I are related to Jesus Christ, our strength and wisdom and peace and joy and love and hope may run out, but His life rushes in to keep us filled to the brim. We are showered with blessings, not because of anything we have or have not done, but simply because of Him.

Anne Graham Lotz

The theme of Proverbs is wisdom, the right use of knowledge. It enables you to evaluate circumstances and people and make the right decisions in life.

Warren Wiersbe

Indeed, wisdom and discernment are among the natural results of a prayer-filled life.

Richard Foster

The more wisdom enters our hearts, the more we will be able to trust our hearts in difficult situations.

John Eldredge

A HEALTHY THOUGHT FOR GARDENERS

Nature's lessons will remain opaque as long as we are full of our own ideas and preconceptions.

Jeff Cox

A GARDENER'S PRAYER

Dear Lord, when I depend upon the world's wisdom, I make many mistakes. But when I trust in Your wisdom, I build my life on a firm foundation. Today and every day I will trust Your Word and follow it, knowing that the ultimate wisdom is Your wisdom and the ultimate truth is Your truth. Amen

The Shepherd's Gift

My cup runs over. Surely goodness and mercy shall follow me all the days of my life; and I will dwell in the house of the Lord forever.

Psalm 23:5-6 NKJV

At harvest time, every gardener hopes for abundance. Sometimes the harvest is bountiful; sometimes it is not. But for Christians who place their lives in the hands of the One from Galilee, the spiritual harvest is always abundant.

Jesus offers life abundant and life eternal. Eternal life is the priceless possession of all who invite Christ into their hearts, but God's abundance is optional: He does not force it upon anyone.

The fullness of life in Christ is available to all who seek it and claim it. Count yourself among that number. Seek first the salvation that is available through a personal relationship with Jesus, and then claim the abundance that can—and should—be yours.

People, places, and things were never meant to give us life. God alone is the author of a fulfilling life.

Gary Smalley & John Trent

God is the giver, and we are the receivers. And His richest gifts are bestowed not upon those who do the greatest things, but upon those who accept His abundance and His grace.

Hannah Whitall Smith

Instead of living a black-and-white existence, we'll be released into a Technicolor world of vibrancy and emotion when we more accurately reflect His nature to the world around us.

Bill Hybels

A TIP FROM THE GARDEN

Nothing is a better lesson in the knowledge of plants than to sit down in front of them and handle them and look them over just as carefully as possible.

Gertrude Jekyll

A GARDENER'S PRAYER

Dear Lord, You have created a world that is glorious to behold yet impossible to comprehend. I praise You for Your creation, Father, and for the sense of awe and wonder that You have placed in my heart. Today, as I venture out to my garden, I will pause to admire Your handiwork. This is the day that You have made, and I will rejoice in it. Amen

He Renews

Do you not know? Have you not heard? The Everlasting God, the LORD, the Creator of the ends of the earth does not become weary or tired. His understanding is inscrutable. He gives strength to the weary, and to him who lacks might He increases power. Though youths grow weary and tired, and vigorous young men stumble badly, yet those who wait for the LORD will gain new strength; they will mount up with wings like eagles, they will run and not get tired, they will walk and not become weary.

Isaiah 40:28–31 NASB

When we genuinely lift our hearts and prayers to God, He renews our strength. Are you almost too weary to lift your head? Then bow it. Offer your concerns and your fears to your Father in Heaven. He is always at your side, offering His love and His strength.

Are you troubled or anxious? Take your anxieties to God in prayer. Are you weak or worried? Delve deeply into God's Holy Word and sense His presence in the quiet moments of the day. Are you spiritually exhausted? Call upon fellow believers to support you, and call upon Christ to renew your spirit and your life. Your Savior will never let you down. To the contrary, He will always lift you up if you ask Him to. So what, dear friend, are you waiting for?

God is not running an antique shop! He is making all things new!

Vance Havner

God specializes in taking bruised, soiled, broken, guilty, and miserable vessels and making them whole, forgiven, and useful again.

Charles Swindoll

The same voice that brought Lazarus out of the tomb raised us to newness of life.

C. H. Spurgeon

A HEALTHY THOUGHT FOR GARDENERS

All of God's earth is holy ground.

Joaquin Miller

A GARDENER'S PRAYER

Heavenly Father, sometimes I am troubled, and sometimes I grow weary. When I am weak, Lord, give me strength. When I am discouraged, renew me. When I am fearful, let me feel Your healing touch. Let me always trust in Your promises, Lord, and let me draw strength from those promises and from Your unending love. Amen

Obey and Be Blessed

By this we know that we have come to know Him, if we keep His commandments.

1 John 2:3 NASB

Oswald Chambers, the author of the Christian classic devotional text, *My Utmost for His Highest*, advised, "Never support an experience which does not have God as its source, and faith in God as its result." These words serve as a powerful reminder that, as Christians, we are called to walk with God and obey His commandments. God gave us His commandments for a reason: so that we might obey them and be blessed.

We live in a world that presents us with countless temptations to stray far from God's path. But, when confronted with sin, we Christians have clear instructions: Walk—or better yet run—in the opposite direction.

To yield to God means to belong to God, and to belong to God means to have all His infinite power. To belong to God means to have all.

Hannah Whitall Smith

Faith, as Paul saw it, was a living, flaming thing leading to surrender and obedience to the commandments of Christ.

A. W. Tozer

Let us remember therefore this lesson: That to worship our God sincerely we must evermore begin by hearkening to His voice, and by giving ear to what He commands us. For if every man goes after his own way, we shall wander. We may well run, but we shall never be a whit nearer to the right way, but rather farther away from it.

John Calvin

True faith commits us to obedience.

A. W. Tozer

A HEALTHY THOUGHT FOR GARDENERS

Let every Christian be a gardener so that he and she and the whole creation which groans in expectation of the Spirit's final harvest, may inherit paradise.

Vigen Guroian

A GARDENER'S PRAYER

Lord, let me live by Your commandments and let me help others do the same. Give me the wisdom to walk righteously in the footsteps of Your Son, Dear Father. And let me place my trust in You, today and forever. Amen

Confidence Restored

I've told you all this so that trusting me, you will be unshakable and assured, deeply at peace. In this godless world you will continue to experience difficulties. But take heart! I've conquered the world.

John 16:33 MSG

Confidence, like a tender seedling, can be nurtured or neglected. Are you a confident, faithful believer, or do you live under a cloud of uncertainty and doubt? As a Christian, you have many reasons to be confident. After all, God is in His heaven; Christ has risen; and you are the recipient of God's grace. Despite these blessings, you may, from time to time, find yourself being tormented by negative emotions—and you are certainly not alone.

Even the most faithful Christians are overcome by occasional bouts of fear and doubt. You are no different. But even when you feel very distant from God, remember that God is never distant from you. When you sincerely seek His presence, He will touch your heart, calm your fears, and restore your confidence.

Bible hope is confidence in the future.

Warren Wiersbe

As I have grown in faith and confidence, I have known more and more that my worth is based on the love of God.

Leslie Williams

Believe and do what God says. The life-changing consequences will be limitless, and the results will be confidence and peace of mind.

Franklin Graham

Jesus gives us the ultimate rest, the confidence we need, to escape the frustration and chaos of the world around us.

Billy Graham

A HEALTHY THOUGHT FOR GARDENERS

Love of gardening is a seed that once sown never dies.

Gertrude Jekyll

A GARDENER'S PRAYER

Lord, You are my Savior and my Sustainer. I will be safe with You in Heaven, and I am safe with You here on earth. Today, I will trust in Your promises, and I will be a confident, obedient, purposeful servant to Your Son. Amen

He Offers Peace

Peace I leave with you; My peace I give to you; not as the world gives do I give to you. Do not let your heart be troubled, nor let it be fearful.

John 14:27 NASB

The best gardens are peaceful places, quiet sanctuaries where their tenders can work and think. The beautiful words of John 14:27 remind us that Jesus offers us peace, not as the world gives, but as He alone gives. Have you found the genuine peace that can be yours through Jesus Christ? Or are you still rushing after the illusion of "peace and happiness" that the world promises but cannot deliver?

Today, as a gift to yourself, to your family, and to your friends, claim the inner peace that is your spiritual birthright: the peace of Jesus Christ. It is offered freely; it has been paid for in full; it is yours for the asking. So ask. And then share.

God cannot give us happiness and peace apart from Himself, because it is not there. There is no such thing.

C. S. Lewis

Peace does not mean to be in a place where there is no noise, trouble, or hard work. Peace means to be in the midst of all those things and still be calm in your heart.

Catherine Marshall

Christ alone can bring lasting peace—peace with God—peace among men and nations—and peace within our hearts.

Billy Graham

God's peace is like a river, not a pond. In other words, a sense of health and well-being, both of which are expressions of the Hebrew shalom, can permeate our homes even when we're in white-water rapids.

Beth Moore

A HEALTHY THOUGHT FOR GARDENERS

A garden is meant to be a place of spiritual repose, stillness, peace, refreshment, and delight.

John Henry Cardinal Newman

A GARDENER'S PRAYER

Dear Lord, I will open my heart to You. And I thank You, God, for Your love, for Your peace, and for Your Son. Amen

Sharing the Good News

Christ did not send me to baptize people but to preach the Good News. And he sent me to preach the Good News without using words of human wisdom so that the cross of Christ would not lose its power.

1 Corinthians 1:17 NCV

I n his second letter to Timothy, Paul offers a message to believers of every generation when he writes, "God has not given us a spirit of timidity" (1:7 NASB). Paul's meaning is crystal clear: When sharing our testimonies, we, as Christians, must be courageous, forthright, and unashamed.

We live in a world that desperately needs the healing message of Christ Jesus. Every believer, each in his or her own way, bears a personal responsibility for sharing that message. If you are a believer in Christ, you know how He has touched your heart and changed your life. Now it's your turn to share the Good News with others. And remember: today is the perfect time to share your testimony because tomorrow may quite simply be too late.

There is nothing anybody else can do that can stop God from using us. We can turn everything into a testimony.

Corrie ten Boom

To stand in an uncaring world and say, "See, here is the Christ" is a daring act of courage.

Calvin Miller

All of God's people are ministers; a few are Ministers with a capital M. We are either good ministers or bad ministers; but ministers we are, and as ministers we shall be judged by the Lord on the Last Day.

Warren Wiersbe

What are God's servants but His minstrels, who must inspire the hearts of men and stir them to spiritual joy!

St. Francis of Assisi

A HEALTHY THOUGHT FOR GARDENERS

I think there are as many kinds of gardening as of poetry.

Joseph Addison

A GARDENER'S PRAYER

Lord, the life that I live and the words that I speak will tell the world how I feel about You. Today and every day, let my testimony be worthy of You. Let my words be sure and true, and let my actions point others to You. Amen

Beyond Guilt

There is therefore now no condemnation to those who are in Christ Jesus, who do not walk according to the flesh, but according to the Spirit.

Romans 8:1 NKJV

All of us have sinned. Sometimes our sins result from our own stubborn rebellion against God's commandments. And sometimes, we are swept up in events that are beyond our abilities to control. Under either set of circumstances, we may experience intense feelings of guilt. But God has an answer for the guilt that we feel. That answer, of course, is His forgiveness. When we confess our wrongdoings and repent from them, we are forgiven by the One who created us.

Are you troubled by feelings of guilt or regret? If so, you must repent from your misdeeds, and you must ask your Heavenly Father for His forgiveness. When you do so, He will forgive you completely and without reservation. Then, you must forgive yourself just as God has forgiven you: thoroughly and unconditionally.

Prayer is essential when a believer is stuck in the pits of unresolved guilt.

Charles Stanley

Let's take Jesus at this word. When he says we're forgiven, let's unload the guilt. When he says we're valuable, let's believe him. When he says we're eternal, let's bury our fear. When he says we're provided for, let's stop worrying.

Max Lucado

Spiritual life without guilt would be like physical life without pain. Guilt is a defense mechanism; it's like an alarm that goes off to lead you to confession when you sin.

John MacArthur

Stop blaming yourself and feeling guilty, unworthy, and unloved. Instead begin to say, "If God is for me, who can be against me? God loves me, and I love myself. Praise the Lord, I am free in Jesus' name, amen!"

Joyce Meyer

A HEALTHY THOUGHT FOR GARDENERS

The best rose-bush, after all, is not that which has the fewest thorns, but that which bears the finest roses.

Henry Van Dyke

A GARDENER'S PRAYER

Dear Lord, thank You for the guilt that I feel when I disobey You. Help me confess my wrongdoings, help me accept Your forgiveness, and help me renew my passion to serve You. Amen

The Morning Watch

Every morning he wakes me. He teaches me to listen like a student. The Lord God helps me learn...

Isaiah 50:4-5 NCV

Each new day is a gift from God, and if you are wise, you will spend a few quiet moments each morning thanking the Giver.

Warren Wiersbe writes, "Surrender your mind to the Lord at the beginning of each day." And that's sound advice. When you begin each day with your head bowed and your heart lifted, you are reminded of God's love, His protection, and His commandments. Then, you can align your priorities for the coming day with the teachings and commandments that God has placed upon your heart.

So, if you've acquired the unfortunate habit of trying to "squeeze" God into the corners of your life, it's time to reshuffle the items on your to-do list by placing God first. And if you haven't already done so, form the habit of spending quality time with your Father in heaven. He deserves it . . . and so do you.

Every morning I spend fifteen minutes filling my mind full of God; and so there's no room left for worry.

Howard Chandler Christy

I suggest you discipline yourself to spend time daily in a systematic reading of God's Word. Make this "quiet time" a priority that nobody can change.

Warren Wiersbe

Knowing God involves an intimate, personal relationship that is developed over time through prayer and getting answers to prayer, through Bible study and applying its teaching to our lives, through obedience and experiencing the power of God, through moment-by-moment submission to Him that results in a moment-by-moment filling of the Holy Spirit.

Anne Graham Lotz

A HEALTHY THOUGHT FOR GARDENERS

Say your prayers in a garden early, ignoring steadfastly the dew, the birds and the flowers, and you will come away overwhelmed by its freshness and joy; go there in order to be overwhelmed.

C. S. Lewis

A GARDENER'S PRAYER

Lord, help me to hear Your direction for my life in the quiet moments of each day. Let everything that I say and do be in Your perfect will. Amen

The Optimistic Gardener

My cup runs over. Surely goodness and mercy shall follow me all the days of my life; and I will dwell in the house of the Lord Forever.

Psalm 23:5-6 NKJV

Gardeners are, by nature, an optimistic lot. They gladly sink money, effort, and time into a plot of ground with no guarantee of return. Planting a garden is truly faith in action.

One of the gardener's most useful tools is a highly cultivated sense of optimism. Why is an upbeat attitude so essential? Because in the garden, there are too many other things to worry about without adding the self-fulfilling prophecy to the list.

So, if you're a gardener—or even if you're not—sow seeds of optimism. They're guaranteed to sprout.

We may run, walk, stumble, drive, or fly, but let us never lose sight of the reason for the journey, or miss a chance to see a rainbow on the way.

Gloria Gaither

The people whom I have seen succeed best in life have always been cheerful and hopeful people who went about their business with a smile on their faces.

Charles Kingsley

Go forward confidently, energetically attacking problems, expecting favorable outcomes.

Norman Vincent Peale

No Christian can be a pessimist, for Christianity is a system of radical optimism.

William Ralph Inge

A HEALTHY THOUGHT FOR GARDENERS

Who bends a knee when violets grow, a hundred secret things shall know.

Rachel Field

A GARDENER'S PRAYER

Dear Lord, today, I will cultivate a positive attitude. I will look for the best in other people, I will expect the best from You, and I will try my best to do my best. Today is a gift, dear Father, and I will treat it that way. Amen

Constant Praise

Through Him then, let us continually offer up a sacrifice of praise to God, that is, the fruit of lips that give thanks to His name.

Hebrews 13:15 NASB

Sometimes, we allow ourselves to become so preoccupied with the demands of daily life that we forget to say "Thank You" to the Giver of all good gifts. But the Bible makes it clear: It pays to praise God.

Worship and praise should be a part of everything we do. Otherwise, we quickly lose perspective as we fall prey to the demands of the moment.

Do you sincerely desire to be a worthy servant of the One who has given you eternal love and eternal life? Then praise Him for who He is and for what He has done for you. Praise Him all day long, every day, for as long as you live . . . and then for all eternity.

Maintaining a focus on God will take our praise to heights that nothing else can.

Jeff Walling

Worship is an act which develops feelings for God, not a feeling for God which is expressed in an act of worship. When we obey the command to praise God in worship, our deep, essential need to be in relationship with God is nurtured.

Eugene Peterson

Be not afraid of saying too much in the praises of God; all the danger is of saying too little.

Matthew Henry

The time for universal praise is sure to come some day. Let us begin to do our part now.

Hannah Whitall Smith

A HEALTHY THOUGHT FOR GARDENERS

Almost any garden, if you see it at just the right moment, can be confused with paradise.

Henry Mitchell

A GARDENER'S PRAYER

Heavenly Father, I come to You today with hope in my heart and praise on my lips. I place my trust in You, Dear Lord, knowing that with You as my Protector, I have nothing to fear. I thank You, Lord, for Your grace, for Your love, and for Your Son. Amen

The Rewards of Diligence

Now the one who plants and the one who waters are equal, and each will receive his own reward according to his own labor.

1 Corinthians 3:8 HCSB

A garden, like so many other things in life, rewards diligence. More often than not, the soil is a fair judge of one's work: the size of one's harvest tends to be proportional to the size of one's efforts.

Thankfully, the work of gardening isn't really work in the strictest sense. The experience of digging in the moist earth is one of nature's sublime pleasures. But make no mistake: in the garden, sublime pleasure and hard work go hand-in-hand.

Gardening may be a labor of love, but it is still labor. The self-tending garden has yet to be invented—hopefully, it never will be. After all, what would a garden be without the work of gardening? A grocery store.

Plough deep while sluggards sleep; and you shall have corn to sell and to keep.

Ben Franklin

Christians are to "labor," which refers to hard, manual work. Hard work is honorable. As Christians we should work hard so that we will have enough to give to those in need, not so that we will have more of what we don't need.

John MacArthur

Thank God every morning when you get up that you have something which must be done, whether you like it or not. Work breeds a hundred virtues that idleness never knows.

Charles Kingsley

Hoping for a good future without investing in today is like a farmer waiting for a crop without ever planting any seed.

John Maxwell

A TIP FROM THE GARDEN

Pray for a good harvest, but continue to hoe.

Old Saying

A GARDENER'S PRAYER

Lord, I know that You desire a bountiful harvest for all Your children. But, You have instructed us that we must sow before we reap, not after. Help me, Lord, to sow the seeds of Your abundance everywhere I go. Let me be diligent in all my undertakings and give me patience to wait for Your harvest. In time, Lord, let me reap the harvest that is found in Your will for my life. Amen

Your Real Riches

He said, "I came naked from my mother's womb, and I will be stripped of everything when I die. The LORD gave me everything I had, and the LORD has taken it away. Praise the name of the LORD!"

Job 1:21 NLT

E arthly riches are transitory; spiritual riches are not. Martin Luther observed, "Many things I have tried to grasp and have lost. That which I have placed in God's hands I still have." How true.

In our demanding world, financial security can be a good thing, but spiritual prosperity is profoundly more important. Certainly we all need the basic necessities of life, but once we've acquired those necessities, enough is enough. Why? Because our real riches are not of this world. We are never really rich until we are rich in spirit.

He is no fool who gives what he cannot keep to gain what he cannot lose.

Jim Elliot

Wealth is something entrusted to us by God, something God doesn't want us to trust. He wants us to trust Him.

Warren Wiersbe

When possessions become our god, we become materialistic and greedy . . . and we forfeit our contentment and our joy.

Charles Swindoll

What we possess often possesses us—we are possessed by possessions.

Oswald Chambers

A HEALTHY THOUGHT FOR GARDENERS

If you have a garden and a library, you have everything you need.

Cicero

A GARDENER'S PRAYER

Dear Lord, all I have belongs to You. When I leave this world I take nothing with me. Help me to value my relationship with You—and my relationships with others—more than I value my material possessions. Amen

A Life of Fulfillment

For You, O God, have tested us; You have refined us as silver is refined . . . we went through fire and through water; but You brought us out to rich fulfillment.

Psalm 66:10–12 NKJV

Everywhere we turn, or so it seems, the world promises fulfillment, contentment, and happiness. But the contentment that the world offers is fleeting and incomplete. Thankfully, the fulfillment that God offers is all encompassing and everlasting.

Sometimes, amid the inevitable hustle and bustle of daily life, we can forfeit—albeit temporarily—the joy of Christ as we wrestle with the challenges of daily living. Yet God's Word is clear: fulfillment through Christ is available to all who seek it and claim it. Count yourself among that number. Seek first a personal, transforming relationship with Jesus, and then claim the joy, the fulfillment, and the spiritual abundance that the Shepherd offers His sheep.

We are never more fulfilled than when our longing for God is met by His presence in our lives.

Billy Graham

Find satisfaction in him who made you, and only then find satisfaction in yourself as part of his creation.

St. Augustine

Our sense of joy, satisfaction, and fulfillment in life increases, no matter what the circumstances, if we are in the center of God's will.

Billy Graham

In serving we uncover the greatest fulfillment within and become a stellar example of a person who knows and loves Jesus.

Vonette Bright

A HEALTHY THOUGHT FOR GARDENERS

Behold! the Holy Grail is found, / Found in each poppy's cup of gold; / And God walks with us as of old.

Joaquin Miller

A GARDENER'S PRAYER

Dear Lord, when I turn my thoughts and prayers to You, I feel peace and fulfillment. But sometimes, when I am distracted by the busyness of the day, fulfillment seems far away. Today, let me trust Your will, let me follow Your commands, and let me accept Your peace. Amen

God Is Love

God is love; and he that dwelleth in love dwelleth in God, and God in him.

1 John 4:16 KJV

The Bible makes this promise: God is love. It's a sweeping statement, a profoundly important description of what God is and how God works. God's love is perfect. When we open our hearts to His perfect love, we are touched by the Creator's hand, and we are transformed.

Today, even if you can only carve out a few quiet moments, offer sincere prayers of thanksgiving to your Creator. He loves you now and throughout all eternity. Open your heart to His presence and His love.

The life of faith is a daily exploration of the constant and countless ways in which God's grace and love are experienced.

Eugene Peterson

Love, for instance, is not something God has which may grow or diminish or cease to be. His love is the way God is, and when He loves He is simply being Himself.

A. W. Tozer

The greatest love of all is God's love for us, a love that showed itself in action.

Billy Graham

If it is maintained that anything so small as the Earth must, in any event, be too unimportant to merit the love of the Creator, we reply that no Christian ever supposed we did merit it. Christ did not die for men because they were intrinsically worth dying for, but because He is intrinsically love, and therefore loves infinitely.

C. S. Lewis

A TIP FROM THE GARDEN

In order to live off the garden, you practically have to live in it.

Kin Hubbard

A GARDENER'S PRAYER

Dear God, You are love. You love me, Father, and I love You. As I love You more, Lord, I am also able to love my family and friends more. I will be Your loving servant, Lord, today and throughout eternity. Amen

Confident Christianity

You are my hope; O Lord GOD, You are my confidence.

Psalm 71:5 NASB

Sometimes, even the most devout Christians can become discouraged. Discouragement, however, is not God's way; He is a God of possibility not negativity. We Christians have many reasons to be confident. God is in His heaven; Christ has risen, and we are the sheep of His flock.

Are you a confident Christian? You should be. God's grace is eternal and His promises are unambiguous. So count your blessings, not your hardships. And live courageously. God is the Giver of all things good, and He watches over you today and forever.

God's omniscience can instill you with a supernatural confidence that can transform your life.

Bill Hybels

If we indulge in any confidence that is not grounded on the Rock of Ages, our confidence is worse than a dream, it will fall on us and cover us with its ruins, causing sorrow and confusion.

C. H. Spurgeon

Jesus gives us the ultimate rest, the confidence we need, to escape the frustration and chaos of the world around us.

Billy Graham

Bible hope is confidence in the future.

Warren Wiersbe

A TIP FROM THE GARDEN

It is a golden maxim to cultivate the garden for the nose, and the eyes will take care of themselves.

Robert Louis Stevenson

A GARDENER'S PRAYER

Lord, when I place my confidence in the things of this earth, I will be disappointed. But, when I put my confidence in You, I am secure. In every aspect of my life, Father, let me place my hope and my trust in Your infinite wisdom and Your boundless grace. Amen

Genuine Contentment

The LORD gives strength to his people; the LORD blesses his people with peace.

Psalm 29:11 NIV

Everywhere we turn, or so it seems, the world promises us contentment and happiness. But the contentment that the world offers is fleeting and incomplete. Thankfully, the contentment that God offers is all encompassing and everlasting.

Happiness depends less upon our circumstances than upon our thoughts. When we turn our thoughts to God, to His gifts, and to His glorious creation, we experience the joy that God intends for His children. But, when we focus on the negative aspects of life—or when we disobey God's commandments—we cause ourselves needless suffering.

Do you sincerely want to be a contented Christian? Then set your mind and your heart upon God's love and His grace . . . and let Him take care of the rest.

Flowers always make people better, happier, and more helpful; they are sunshine, food and medicine for the soul.

Luther Burbank

Contentment is something we learn by adhering to the basics—cultivating a growing relationship with Jesus Christ, living daily, and knowing that Christ strengthens us for every challenge.

Charles Stanley

I believe that in every time and place it is within our power to acquiesce in the will of God—and what peace it brings to do so!

Elisabeth Elliot

The secret of contentment in the midst of change is found in having roots in the changeless Christ—the same yesterday, today and forever.

Ed Young

A TIP FROM THE GARDEN

The best place to seek God is in a garden. You can dig for him there.

George Bernard Shaw

A GARDENER'S PRAYER

Dear Lord, You offer me contentment and peace; let me accept Your peace. Help me to trust Your Word, to follow Your commandments, and to welcome the peace of Jesus into my heart, today and forever. Amen

Giving Thanks for God's Word

For I am not ashamed of the gospel, because it is God's power for salvation to everyone who believes.

Romans 1:16 HCSB

God's Word is unlike any other book. A. W. Tozer wrote, "The purpose of the Bible is to bring men to Christ, to make them holy and prepare them for heaven. In this it is unique among books, and it always fulfills its purpose."

George Mueller observed, "The vigor of our spiritual lives will be in exact proportion to the place held by the Bible in our lives and in our thoughts." As Christians, we are called upon to study God's Holy Word and then to share it with the world.

The Bible is a priceless gift, a tool for Christians to use as they share the Good News of their Savior, Christ Jesus. Too many Christians, however, keep their spiritual tool kits tightly closed and out of sight. Jonathan Edwards advised, "Be assiduous in reading the Holy Scriptures. This is the fountain whence all knowledge in divinity must be derived. Therefore let not this treasure lie by you neglected." God's Holy Word is, indeed, a priceless, one-of-a-kind treasure. Handle it with care, but, more importantly, handle it every day.

The instrument of our sanctification is the Word of God. The Spirit of God brings to our minds the precepts and doctrines of truth, and applies them with power. The truth is our sanctifier. If we do not hear or read it, we will not grow in sanctification.

C. H. Spurgeon

God gives us a compass and a Book of promises and principles—the Bible—and lets us make our decisions day by day as we sense the leading of His Spirit. This is how we grow.

Warren Wiersbe

The Bible is a remarkable commentary on perspective. Through its divine message, we are brought face to face with issues and tests in daily living and how, by the power of the Holy Spirit, we are enabled to respond positively to them.

Luci Swindoll

A HEALTHY THOUGHT FOR GARDENERS

The hills are mute, but how they speak of God!

Charles Hansom Towne

A GARDENER'S PRAYER

Dear Lord, the Bible is Your gift to me. Let me use it, let me trust it, and let me obey it, today and every day that I live. Amen

The Power of Words

Watch the way you talk. Let nothing foul or dirty come out of your mouth. Say only what helps, each word a gift.

Ephesians 4:29 MSG

A lasting relationship, like a bountiful garden, must be tended with care. The words that we speak have the power to do great good or great harm. If we speak words of encouragement and hope, we can lift others up. And that's exactly what God commands us to do!

Sometimes, when we feel uplifted and secure, it is easy to speak kind words. Other times, when we are discouraged or tired, we can scarcely summon the energy to uplift ourselves, much less anyone else. God intends that we speak words of kindness, wisdom, and truth, no matter our circumstances, no matter our emotions. When we do, we share a priceless gift with the world, and we give glory to the One who gave His life for us. As believers, we must do no less.

The truest help we can render an afflicted man is not to take his burden from him, but to call out his best energy, that he may be able to bear the burden himself.

Phillips Brooks

Isn't it funny the way some combinations of words can give you—almost apart from their meaning—a thrill like music?

C. S. Lewis

A kind word of praise, of sympathy, of encouragement; it costs us so little, yet how often does pride or envy or indifference prevent us from speaking it?

Frederic W. Farrar

No journey is complete that does not lead through some dark valleys. We can properly comfort others only with the comfort we ourselves have been given by God.

Vance Havner

A TIP FROM THE GARDEN

One of the most important things a gardener does is look. The rewards are immeasurable.

Elsa Bakalar

A GARDENER'S PRAYER

Lord, help me cultivate kindness wherever I go. Make me a powerful source of encouragement to those in need, and let my words and deeds be worthy of Your Son, the One who gives me courage and strength for this day and for all eternity. Amen

Acceptance Today

I have learned to be content whatever the circumstances.

Philippians 4:11 NIV

Are you embittered by a personal tragedy that you did not deserve and cannot understand? If so, it's time to accept the unchangeable past and to have faith in the promise of tomorrow. It's time to trust God completely—and it's time to reclaim the peace—His peace—that can and should be yours.

On occasion, you will be confronted with situations that you simply don't understand. But God does. And He has a reason for everything that He does.

God doesn't explain Himself in ways that we, as mortals with limited insight and clouded vision, can comprehend. So, instead of understanding every aspect of God's unfolding plan for our lives and our universe, we must be satisfied to trust Him completely. We cannot know God's motivations, nor can we understand His actions. We can, however, trust Him, and we must.

Faith is the willingness to receive whatever he wants to give, or the willingness not to have what he does not want to give.

Elisabeth Elliot

The key to contentment is to consider. Consider who you are and be satisfied with that. Consider what you have and be satisfied with that. Consider what God's doing and be satisfied with that.

Luci Swindoll

We need to be at peace with our past, content with our present, and sure about our future, knowing they are all in God's hands.

Joyce Meyer

I have held many things in my hands, and I have lost them all; but whatever I have placed in God's hands, that I still possess.

Corrie ten Boom

A HEALTHY THOUGHT FOR GARDENERS

One of the most soothing sounds of nature is the laughter of falling water.

Jeff Cox

A GARDENER'S PRAYER

Heavenly Father, thank You for the abundant life that is mine through Christ. Give me courage, Lord, to claim the spiritual riches that You have promised, and lead me according to Your plan for my life, today and always. Amen

Choosing Wisely

But the wisdom that is from above is first pure, then peaceable, gentle, willing to yield, full of mercy and good fruits, without partiality and without hypocrisy.

James 3:17 NKJV

Because we are creatures of free will, we make choices—lots of them. When we make choices that are pleasing to our Heavenly Father, we are blessed. When we make choices that cause us to walk in the footsteps of God's Son, we enjoy the abundance that Christ has promised to those who follow Him. But when we make choices that are displeasing to God, we sow seeds that have the potential to bring forth a bitter harvest.

Today, as you encounter the challenges of everyday living, you will make hundreds of choices. Choose wisely. Make your thoughts and your actions pleasing to God. And remember: every choice that is displeasing to Him is the wrong choice—no exceptions.

Life is a series of choices between the bad, the good, and the best. Everything depends on how we choose.

Vance Havner

We are either the masters or the victims of our attitudes. It is a matter of personal choice. Who we are today is the result of choices we made yesterday. Tomorrow, we will become what we choose today. To change means to choose to change.

John Maxwell

Good and evil both increase at compound interest. That is why the little decisions you and I make every day are of such infinite importance.

C. S. Lewis

God expresses His love in giving us the freedom to choose.

Charles Stanley

A TIP FROM THE GARDEN

One should learn also to enjoy the neighbor's garden, however small; the roses straggling over the fence, the scent of lilacs drifting across the road.

Henry Van Dyke

A GARDENER'S PRAYER

Dear Lord, help me cultivate a positive attitude, and, help me focus my thoughts on Your will for my life. Today, I will strive to make decisions that are pleasing to You, and I will strive to follow in the footsteps of Your Son. Amen

We Are All Role Models

You are the light that gives light to the world . . . . In the same way, you should be a light for other people. Live so that they will see the good things you do and will praise your Father in heaven.

Matthew 5:14, 16 NCV

Whether we like it or not, we are role models. Hopefully, the lives we lead and the choices we make will serve as enduring examples of the spiritual abundance that is available to all who worship God and obey His commandments.

Ask yourself this question: Are you the kind of role model whom you would want to emulate? If so, congratulations. But if certain aspects of your behavior could stand improvement, the best day to begin your self-improvement regimen is this one. Because whether you realize it or not, people you love are watching your behavior, and they're learning how to live. You owe it to them—and to yourself—to live righteously and well.

Our walk counts far more than our talk, always!

George Mueller

A man ought to live so that everybody knows he is a Christian, and most of all, his family ought to know.

D. L. Moody

Let us preach you, Dear Jesus, without preaching, not by words but by our example, by the casting force, the sympathetic influence of what we do, the evident fullness of the love our hearts bear to you. Amen.

Mother Teresa

We are to leave an impression on all those we meet that communicates whose we are and what kingdom we represent.

Lisa Bevere

A HEALTHY THOUGHT FOR GARDENERS

One who plants a garden, plants happiness.

Old Saying

A GARDENER'S PRAYER

Dear Lord, help me be an honorable role model to others. Let the things that I say and the things that I do show everyone what it means to be a follower of Your Son. Amen

Heeding God's Call

One thing I do, forgetting those things which are behind and reaching forward to those things which are ahead, I press toward the goal for the prize of the upward call of God in Christ Jesus.

Philippians 3:13-14 NKJV

It is vitally important that you heed God's call. In John 15:16, Jesus says, "You did not choose me, but I chose you and appointed you to go and bear fruit—fruit that will last" (NIV). In other words, you have been called by Christ, and now, it is up to you to decide precisely how you will answer.

Have you already found your special calling? If so, you're a very lucky person. If not, keep searching and keep praying until you discover it. And remember this: God has important work for you to do—work that no one else on earth can accomplish but you.

The place where God calls you is the place where your deep gladness and the world's deep hunger meet.

Frederick Buechner

Faith does not concern itself with the entire journey. One step is enough.

Mrs. Charles E. Cowman

When you become consumed by God's call on your life, everything will take on new meaning and significance. You will begin to see every facet of your life, including your pain, as a means through which God can work to bring others to Himself.

Charles Stanley

The Bible teaches that God has considered man a working partner.

Billy Graham

A HEALTHY THOUGHT FOR GARDENERS
He who plants a garden works hand in hand with God.

Malloch

A GARDENER'S PRAYER
Heavenly Father, You have called me to Your kingdom work, and I acknowledge that calling. In these quiet moments before this busy day unfolds, I come to You. I will study Your Word and seek Your guidance. Give me the wisdom to know Your will for my life and the courage to follow wherever You may lead me, today and forever. Amen

His Perspective . . . and Yours

Since you have been raised to new life with Christ, set your sights on the realities of heaven, where Christ sits at God's right hand in the place of honor and power.

Colossians 3:1 NLT

Tending a garden helps you maintain perspective. When the events of life seem out of balance, your garden is the perfect place to vanquish the stresses and strains of everyday living. And, of course, your garden is a wonderful place to remind yourself of God's timeless truths.

Today, as you survey that little patch of ground that God has entrusted to your care, take time to ponder the wisdom of God's unchanging Word. The wisdom of the world changes with the ever-shifting sands of public opinion. God's wisdom does not. His wisdom is eternal. It never changes. And it most certainly is the wisdom that you must use to plan your day, your life, and your eternal destiny.

The proper perspective creates within us a spirit of reaching outside of ourselves with joy and enthusiasm.

Luci Swindoll

Instead of being frustrated and overwhelmed by all that is going on in our world, go to the Lord and ask Him to give you His eternal perspective.

Kay Arthur

When we look at the individual parts of our lives, some things appear unfair and unpleasant. When we take them out of the context of the big picture, we easily drift into the attitude that we deserve better, and the tumble down into the pit of pride begins.

Susan Hunt

A HEALTHY THOUGHT FOR GARDENERS

An hour's hard digging is a good way of getting one's mind back in the right perspective.

Richard Briers

A GARDENER'S PRAYER

Lord, sometimes, the world's perspective can lead me astray. Sometimes I become confused; sometimes, in the busyness of my daily life, I lose perspective. Help me, Lord, to see the world through Your eyes. Give me guidance and wisdom and perspective. Lead me according to Your plan for my life and according to Your commandments. And keep me ever mindful, Father, that Your reality is the ultimate reality, and that Your truth is the ultimate truth, now and forever. Amen

Genuine Peace

These things I have spoken to you, that in Me you may have peace. In the world you will have tribulation; but be of good cheer, I have overcome the world.

John 16:33 NKJV

When, in the quiet early morning hours, we sink our hands into God's good earth, all seems right with the world. Does everything seem right in your world? Have you found the genuine peace that can be yours through Jesus Christ? Or are you still rushing after the illusion of "peace and happiness" that the world promises but cannot deliver?

The beautiful words of John 16:33 remind us that Jesus offers us peace, not as the world gives, but as He alone gives. Our challenge is to accept Christ's peace into our hearts and then, as best we can, to share His peace with our neighbors.

Today, as a gift to yourself, to your family, and to your friends, claim the inner peace that is your spiritual birth-right: the peace of Jesus Christ. It is offered freely; it has been paid for in full; it is yours for the asking. So ask. And then share.

We will never be happy until we make God the source of our fulfillment and the answer to our longings.

Stormie Omartian

The peace that Jesus gives is never engineered by circumstances on the outside.

Oswald Chambers

Working in the garden gives me something beyond the enjoyment of the senses. It gives me a profound feeling of inner peace.

Ruth Stout

A HEALTHY THOUGHT FOR GARDENERS

Gardening is a labour full of tranquility and satisfaction; natural and instructive, and as such contributes to the most serious contemplation, experience, health and longevity.

John Evelyn

A GARDENER'S PRAYER

Dear Lord, whether I am in the garden or not, let me accept the peace and abundance that You offer through Your Son Jesus. You are the Giver of all things good, Father, and You give me peace when I draw close to You. Help me to trust Your will, to follow Your commands, and to accept Your peace, today and forever. Amen

Making Peace with Your Past

The Lord says, "Forget what happened before, and do not think about the past. Look at the new thing I am going to do. It is already happening. Don't you see it? I will make a road in the desert and rivers in the dry land."

Isaiah 43:18-19 NCV

Because you are human, you may be slow to forget yesterday's disappointments. But, if you sincerely seek to focus your hopes and energies on the future, then you must find ways to accept the past, no matter how difficult it may be to do so.

Have you made peace with your past? If so, congratulations. But, if you are mired in the quicksand of regret, it's time to plan your escape. How can you do so? By accepting what has been and by trusting God for what will be.

So, if you have not yet made peace with the past, today is the day to declare an end to all hostilities. When you do, you can then turn your thoughts to wondrous promises of God and to the glorious future that He has in store for you.

The pages of your past cannot be rewritten, but the pages of your tomorrows are blank.

Zig Ziglar

The wise man gives proper appreciation in his life to his past. He learns to sift the sawdust of heritage in order to find the nuggets that make the current moment have any meaning.

Grady Nutt

Shake the dust from your past, and move forward in His promises.

Kay Arthur

Our yesterdays teach us how to savor our todays and tomorrows.

Patsy Clairmont

A HEALTHY THOUGHT FOR GARDENERS

All my hurts my garden spade can heal.

Ralph Waldo Emerson

A GARDENER'S PRAYER

Heavenly Father, free me from anger, resentment, and envy. When I am bitter, I cannot feel the peace that You intend for my life. Keep me mindful that forgiveness is Your commandment, and help me accept the past, treasure the present, and trust the future . . . to You. Amen

Pleasing God

But neither exile nor homecoming is the main thing. Cheerfully pleasing God is the main thing, and that's what we aim to do, regardless of our conditions.

2 Corinthians 5:9 MSG

When God made you, He equipped you with an array of talents and abilities that are uniquely yours. It's up to you to discover those talents and to use them, but sometimes the world will encourage you to do otherwise. At times, society will attempt to cubbyhole you, to standardize you, and to make you fit into a particular, preformed mold. Sometimes, because you're an imperfect human being, you may become so wrapped up in meeting society's expectations that you fail to focus on God's expectations. To do so is a mistake of major proportions—don't make it.

Who will you try to please today: God or man? Your primary obligation is not to please imperfect men and women. Your obligation is to strive diligently to meet the expectations of an all-knowing and perfect God. Trust Him always. Love Him always. Praise Him always. And seek to please Him. Always.

It is impossible to please God doing things motivated by and produced by the flesh.

Bill Bright

God is not hard to please. He does not expect us to be absolutely perfect. He just expects us to keep moving toward Him and believing in Him, letting Him work with us to bring us into conformity to His will and ways.

Joyce Meyer

All our offerings, whether music or martyrdom, are like the intrinsically worthless present of a child, which a father values indeed, but values only for the intention.

C. S. Lewis

A HEALTHY THOUGHT FOR GARDENERS

We have no time to sin when we devote our time to working in the garden with God.

Jim G. Brown

A GARDENER'S PRAYER

Dear Lord, today I will honor You with my thoughts, my actions, and my prayers. I will seek to please You, and I will strive to serve You. Your blessings are as limitless as Your love. And because I have been so richly blessed, I will worship You, Father, with thanksgiving in my heart and praise on my lips, this day and forever. Amen

Prayer Changes Things and You

And everything—whatever you ask in prayer, believing—you will receive.

Matthew 21:22 HCSB

Jesus made it clear to His disciples: they should pray always. And so should we. Genuine, heartfelt prayer changes things and it changes us. When we lift our hearts to our Father in heaven, we open ourselves to a never-ending source of divine wisdom and infinite love.

Do you have questions that you simply can't answer? Ask for the guidance of your Father in heaven. Do you sincerely seek the gift of everlasting love and eternal life? Accept the grace of God's only begotten Son. Whatever your need, no matter how great or small, pray about it. Instead of waiting for mealtimes or bedtimes, follow the instruction of your Savior: pray always and never lose heart. And remember: God is not just near; He is here, and He's ready to talk with you. Now!

You don't need fancy words or religious phrases. Just tell God the way it really is.

Jim Cymbala

We must pray literally without ceasing, in every occurrence and employment of our lives. You know I mean that prayer of the heart which is independent of place or situation, or which is, rather, a habit of lifting up the heart to God, as in a constant communication with Him.

Elizabeth Ann Seton

I need the spiritual revival that comes from spending quiet time alone with Jesus in prayer and in thoughtful meditation on His Word.

Anne Graham Lotz

Prayer moves the arm that moves the world.

Annie Armstrong

A HEALTHY THOUGHT FOR GARDENERS

Adam was a gardener, and God who made him sees that half a proper gardener's work is done upon his knees.

Rudyard Kipling

A GARDENER'S PRAYER

I pray to You, my Heavenly Father, because You desire it and because I need it. Prayer not only changes things, it changes me. Help me, Lord, never to face the demands of the day without first spending time with You. Amen

Beyond Bitterness

Don't insist on getting even; that's not for you to do. "I'll do the judging," says God. "I'll take care of it."

Romans 12:19 MSG

Bitterness is a spiritual sickness. It will consume your soul; it is dangerous to your emotional health. It can destroy you if you let it . . . so don't let it!

If you are caught up in intense feelings of anger or resentment, you know all too well the destructive power of these emotions. How can you rid yourself of these feelings? First, you must prayerfully ask God to cleanse your heart. Then, you must learn to catch yourself whenever thoughts of bitterness or hatred begin to attack you. Your challenge is this: You must learn to resist negative thoughts before they hijack your emotions.

Matthew 5:22 teaches us that if we judge our brothers and sisters, we, too, will be subject to judgement. Let us refrain, then, from judging our neighbors. Instead, let us forgive them and love them, while leaving their judgement to a far more capable authority: the One who sits on His throne in heaven.

Revenge is the raging fire that consumes the arsonist.

Max Lucado

Bitterness is a spiritual cancer, a rapidly growing malignancy that can consume your life. Bitterness cannot be ignored but must be healed at the very core, and only Christ can heal bitterness.

Beth Moore

Be patient and understanding. Life is too short to be vengeful or malicious.

Phillips Brooks

Forgiveness is the key that unlocks the door of resentment and the handcuffs of hate. It is a power that breaks the chains of bitterness and the shackles of selfishness.

Corrie ten Boom

A HEALTHY THOUGHT FOR GARDENERS
Never does nature say one thing and wisdom another.

Juvenal

A GARDENER'S PRAYER
Dear Lord, free me from the poison of bitterness and the futility of blame. Let me turn away from destructive emotions so that I may know the perfect peace and the spiritual abundance that can, and should, be mine. Amen

Unbending Truth

*So put away all falsehood and "tell your neighbor the truth"
because we belong to each other.*

Ephesians 4:25 NLT

O swald Chambers advised, "Never support an experience which does not have God as its source, and faith in God as its result." These words serve as a powerful reminder that as Christians we are called to walk with God and to obey His commandments. But, we live in a world that presents us with countless temptations to wander far from God's path. These temptations have the potential to destroy us, in part, because they cause us to be dishonest with ourselves and with others.

Dishonesty is a habit. Once we start bending the truth, we're likely to keep bending it. A far better strategy, of course, is to acquire the habit of being completely forthright with God, with other people, and with ourselves.

Honesty is also a habit, a habit that pays powerful dividends for those who place character above convenience. So, the next time you're tempted to bend the truth—or to break it—ask yourself this simple question: "What does God want me to do?" Then listen carefully to your conscience. When you do, your actions will be honorable, and your character will take care of itself.

A person's character is determined by his motives, and motive is always a matter of the heart.

John Eldredge

Right actions done for the wrong reason do not help to build the internal quality of character called a "virtue," and it is this quality or character that really matters.

C. S. Lewis

God never called us to naïveté. He called us to integrity. The biblical concept of integrity emphasizes mature innocence not childlike ignorance.

Beth Moore

The highest reward for man's toil is not what he gets for it but what he becomes by it.

John Ruskin

A HEALTHY THOUGHT FOR GARDENERS

Nature and the garden bring out the best in our characters.

Felicity Bryan

A GARDENER'S PRAYER

Heavenly Father, help me see the truth, help me speak the truth, and help me live the truth—today and every day of my life. Amen

Working for the Harvest

The thing you should want most is God's kingdom and doing what God wants. Then all these other things you need will be given to you.

Matthew 6:33 NCV

If you're a disciplined gardener, then you know that the job of tending your little patch of ground requires work and plenty of it. But God is not complaining, and neither should you.

God's Holy Word is clear: He expects His children to do the work first and reap the harvest second. So, whether you're in the garden or outside it, your success will depend, in large part, upon the quality and quantity of your work.

Our Heavenly Father has created a world in which hard work is honored and idleness is not. We reside in that world, so we should live—and we should garden—accordingly.

I am more and more persuaded that all that is required of us is faithful seed-sowing. The harvest is bound to follow.

Annie Armstrong

The evangelistic harvest is always urgent. The destiny of men and of nations is always being decided. Every generation is strategic. We are not responsible for the past generation, and we cannot bear the full responsibility for the next one, but we do have our generation. God will hold us responsible as to how well we fulfill our responsibilities to this age and take advantage of our opportunities.

Billy Graham

Every day, I find countless opportunities to decide whether I will obey God and demonstrate my love for Him or try to please myself or the world system. God is waiting for my choices.

Bill Bright

A HEALTHY THOUGHT FOR GARDENERS

A man's mind may be likened to a garden, which may be intelligently cultivated or allowed to run wild; but whether cultivated or neglected, it must, and will, bring forth.

James Allen

A GARDENER'S PRAYER

Dear Lord, You have given me another day of life. Today, let me be successful in Your eyes. Help me, Father, see more clearly the path You have chosen for me. Enable me to sow, to reap, and to give thanks for Your creation, for Your love, and for Your Son. Amen

Focusing on God

Give your entire attention to what God is doing right now, and don't get worked up about what may or may not happen tomorrow. God will help you deal with whatever hard things come up when the time comes.

Matthew 6:34 MSG

All of us may find our courage tested by the inevitable disappointments and tragedies of life. After all, ours is a world filled with uncertainty, hardship, sickness, and danger. Trouble, it seems, is never too far from the front door.

When we focus upon our fears and our doubts, we may find many reasons to lie awake at night and fret about the uncertainties of the coming day. A better strategy, of course, is to focus not upon our fears, but instead upon our God.

God is as near as your next breath, and He is in control. He offers salvation to all His children, including you. God is your shield and your strength; you are His forever. So don't focus your thoughts upon the fears of the day. Instead, trust God's plan and His eternal love for you. And remember: God is good, and He has the last word.

His hand on me is a father's hand, gently guiding and encouraging. His hand lets me know he is with me, so I am not afraid.

Mary Morrison Suggs

Whether our fear is absolutely realistic or out of proportion in our minds, our greatest refuge is Jesus Christ.

Luci Swindoll

Fear and doubt are conquered by a faith that rejoices. And faith can rejoice because the promises of God are as certain as God Himself.

Kay Arthur

A HEALTHY THOUGHT FOR GARDENERS

Once you've finalized your plan, it's time to get your hands dirty.

Burpee Complete Gardener

A GARDENER'S PRAYER

Your Word reminds me, Lord, that even when I walk through the valley of the shadow of death, I need fear no evil, for You are with me, and You comfort me. Thank You, Lord, for a perfect love that casts out fear. Let me live courageously and faithfully this day and every day. Amen

Commissioned to Witness

Therefore go and make disciples of all nations, baptizing them in the name of the Father and of the Son and of the Holy Spirit, and teaching them to obey everything I have commanded you. And surely I am with you always, to the very end of the age.

Matthew 28:19-20 NIV

After His resurrection, Jesus addressed His disciples. As recorded in the 28th chapter of Matthew, Christ instructed His followers to share His message with the world. This "Great Commission" applies to Christians of every generation, including our own.

As believers, we are called to share the Good News of Jesus with our families, with our neighbors, and with the world. Christ commanded His disciples to become fishers of men. We must do likewise, and we must do so today. Tomorrow may indeed be too late.

Our commission is quite specific. We are told to be His witness to all nations. For us, as His disciples, to refuse any part of this commission frustrates the love of Jesus Christ, the Son of God.

Catherine Marshall

Witnessing is not something that we do for the Lord; it is something that He does through us if we are filled with the Holy Spirit.

Warren Wiersbe

In their heart of hearts, I think all true followers of Christ long to become contagious Christians. Though unsure about how to do so or the risks involved, deep down they sense that there isn't anything as rewarding as opening a person up to God's love and truth.

Bill Hybels

A HEALTHY THOUGHT FOR GARDENERS

Put in the plow and plant the great hereafter in the now.

Robert Browning

A GARDENER'S PRAYER

Heavenly Father, every man and woman, every boy and girl is Your child. You desire that all Your children know Jesus as their Lord and Savior. Father, let me be part of Your Great Commission. Let me give, let me pray, and let me go out into this world so that I might be a fisher of men . . . for You. Amen

MORE FROM GOD'S WORD
PATIENCE

It takes patience to be a good gardener. The following passages remind us that patience is, indeed, a virtue.

Knowing God leads to self-control. Self-control leads to patient endurance, and patient endurance leads to godliness.

2 Peter 1:6 NLT

Patience and encouragement come from God. And I pray that God will help you all agree with each other the way Christ Jesus wants.

Romans 15:5 NCV

But if we look forward to something we don't have yet, we must wait patiently and confidently.

Romans 8:25 NLT

Now we exhort you, brethren, warn those who are unruly, comfort the fainthearted, uphold the weak, be patient with all.

1 Thessalonians 5:14 NKJV

God has chosen you and made you his holy people. He loves you. So always do these things: Show mercy to others, be kind, humble, gentle, and patient.

Colossians 3:12 NCV

And the servant of the Lord must not strive; but be gentle unto all men, apt to teach, patient; in meekness instructing those that oppose themselves....

2 Timothy 2:24-25 KJV

The Lord is wonderfully good to those who wait for him and seek him. So it is good to wait quietly for salvation from the Lord.

Lamentations 3:25-26 NLT

Wait on the LORD; be of good courage, and He shall strengthen your heart; wait, I say, on the LORD!

Psalm 27:14 NKJV

Wherefore seeing we also are compassed about with so great a cloud of witnesses, let us lay aside every weight, and the sin which doth so easily beset us, and let us run with patience the race that is set before us....

Hebrews 12:1 KJV

When it comes to gardening, hard work pays big dividends, as the following verses will attest.

Whatever you do, do it enthusiastically, as something done for the Lord and not for men.

Colossians 3:23 HCSB

Whatever your hands find to do, do with [all] your strength.

Ecclesiastes 9:10 HCSB

He did it with all his heart. So he prospered.

2 Chronicles 31:21 NKJV

Cast your burden on the Lord, and He shall sustain you; He shall never permit the righteous to be moved.

Psalm 55:22 NKJV

Do not lack diligence; be fervent in spirit; serve the Lord.

Romans 12:11 HCSB

We must do the works of Him who sent Me while it is day. Night is coming when no one can work.

John 9:4 HCSB

Lazy people's desire for sleep will kill them, because they refuse to work. All day long they wish for more, but good people give without holding back.

Proverbs 21:25-26 NKJV

In fact, when we were with you, this is what we commanded you: "If anyone isn't willing to work, he should not eat."

2 Thessalonians 3:10 HCSB

Don't work only while being watched, in order to please men, but as slaves of Christ, do God's will from your heart. Render service with a good attitude, as to the Lord and not to men.

Ephesians 6:6-7 HCSB

Whether you're in the garden, or anywhere else, it pays to be grateful.

Thanks be to God for His indescribable gift.

2 Corinthians 9:15 HCSB

And let the peace of the Messiah, to which you were also called in one body, control your hearts. Be thankful.

Colossians 3:15 HCSB

Therefore as you have received Christ Jesus the Lord, walk in Him, rooted and built up in Him and established in the faith, just as you were taught, and overflowing with thankfulness.

Colossians 2:6-7 HCSB

It is good to give thanks to the Lord, and to sing praises to Your name, O Most High.

Psalm 92:1 NKJV

Enter into His gates with thanksgiving, and into His courts with praise. Be thankful to Him, and bless His name. For the Lord is good; His mercy is everlasting, and His truth endures to all generations.

Psalm 100:4-5 NKJV

And whatever you do, in word or in deed, do everything in the name of the Lord Jesus, giving thanks to God the Father through Him.

Colossians 3:17 HCSB

In everything give thanks; for this is the will of God in Christ Jesus for you.

1 Thessalonians 5:18 NKJV

God wants you to cultivate your talents; your intentions should be the same.

Do not neglect the gift that is in you.

1 Timothy 4:14 HCSB

Each one has his own gift from God, one in this manner and another in that.

1 Corinthians 7:7 NKJV

So he who had received five talents came and brought five other talents, saying, "Lord, you delivered to me five talents; look, I have gained five more talents besides them." His lord said to him, "Well done, good and faithful servant; you were faithful over a few things, I will make you ruler over many things. Enter into the joy of your lord."

Matthew 25:20-21 NKJV

I remind you to keep ablaze the gift of God that is in you.

2 Timothy 1:6 HCSB

Based on the gift they have received, everyone should use it to serve others, as good managers of the varied grace of God.

1 Peter 4:10 HCSB

According to the grace given to us, we have different gifts: If prophecy, use it according to the standard of faith; if service, in service; if teaching, in teaching; if exhorting, in exhortation; giving, with generosity; leading, with diligence; showing mercy, with cheerfulness.

Romans 12:6-8 HCSB

Whatever you do, do it enthusiastically, as something done for the Lord and not for men.

Colossians 3:23 HCSB

When you sow seeds of righteousness, you will reap a bountiful harvest.

The righteous one will live by his faith.

Habakkuk 2:4 HCSB

Sow righteousness for yourselves and reap faithful love; break up your untilled ground. It is time to seek the Lord until He comes and sends righteousness on you like the rain.

Hosea 10:12 HCSB

And now, Israel, what does the Lord your God ask of you except to fear the Lord your God by walking in all His ways, to love Him, and to worship the Lord your God with all your heart and all your soul?

Deuteronomy 10:12 HCSB

And the world is passing away, and the lust of it; but he who does the will of God abides forever.

1 John 2:17 NKJV

Because the eyes of the Lord are on the righteous and His ears are open to their request. But the face of the Lord is against those who do evil.

1 Peter 3:12 HCSB

Flee from youthful passions, and pursue righteousness, faith, love, and peace, along with those who call on the Lord from a pure heart.

2 Timothy 2:22 HCSB

Do what is right and good in the Lord's sight, so that you may prosper and so that you may enter and possess the good land the Lord your God swore to [give] your fathers.

Deuteronomy 6:18 HCSB

When it's time to renew your spirits, you can return to your garden . . . and to God.

But may the God of all grace, who called us to His eternal glory by Christ Jesus, after you have suffered a while, perfect, establish, strengthen, and settle you.

1 Peter 5:10 NKJV

Finally, brothers, rejoice. Be restored, be encouraged, be of the same mind, be at peace, and the God of love and peace will be with you.

2 Corinthians 13:11 HCSB

But those who wait on the Lord shall renew their strength; They shall mount up with wings like eagles, they shall run and not be weary, they shall walk and not faint.

Isaiah 40:31 NKJV

I will give you a new heart and put a new spirit within you.

Ezekiel 36:26 HCSB

Therefore if anyone is in Christ, he is a new creature; the old things passed away; behold, new things have come.

2 Corinthians 5:17 HCSB

You are being renewed in the spirit of your minds; you put on the new man, the one created according to God's likeness in righteousness and purity of the truth.

Ephesians 4:23-24 HCSB

Then the One seated on the throne said, "Look! I am making everything new."

Revelation 21:5 HCSB

Prayer changes everything, including you. So pray.

The intense prayer of the righteous is very powerful.

James 5:16 HCSB

Let the words of my mouth and the meditation of my heart be acceptable in Your sight, O Lord, my strength and my Redeemer.

Psalm 19:14 NKJV

Yet He often withdrew to deserted places and prayed.

Luke 5:16 HCSB

Don't worry about anything, but in everything, through prayer and petition with thanksgiving, let your requests be made known to God.

Philippians 4:6 HCSB

Rejoice in hope; be patient in affliction; be persistent in prayer.

Romans 12:12 HCSB

Ask, and it shall be given you; seek, and ye shall find; knock, and it shall be opened unto you: for every one that asketh receiveth; and he that seeketh findeth; and to him that knocketh it shall be opened.

Matthew 7:7-8 KJV

Is anyone among you suffering? He should pray. Is anyone cheerful? He should sing praises.

James 5:13 HCSB

Gardening is an exercise in perseverance. And, perseverance pays, as the following verses clearly demonstrate.

Let us not become weary in doing good, for at the proper time we will reap a harvest if we do not give up.

Galatians 6:9 NIV

For you have need of endurance, so that when you have done the will of God, you may receive what was promised.

Hebrews 10:36 NASB

It is better to finish something than to start it. It is better to be patient than to be proud.

Ecclesiastes 7:8 NCV

Let us lay aside every weight and the sin that so easily ensnares us, and run with endurance the race that lies before us, keeping our eyes on Jesus, the source and perfecter of our faith.

Hebrews 12:1-2 HCSB

Do you not know that the runners in a stadium all race, but only one receives the prize? Run in such a way that you may win. Now everyone who competes exercises self-control in everything. However, they do it to receive a perishable crown, but we an imperishable one.

1 Corinthians 9:24-25 HCSB

But as for you, be strong; don't be discouraged, for your work has a reward.

2 Chronicles 15:7 HCSB

I have fought the good fight, I have finished the race, I have kept the faith.

2 Timothy 4:7 HCSB

Now we want each of you to demonstrate the same diligence for the final realization of your hope, so that you won't become lazy, but imitators of those who inherit the promises through faith and perseverance.

Hebrews 6:11-12 HCSB

Optimistic gardeners are good gardeners. These verses remind us that the future is bright for those who believe.

For God has not given us a spirit of fearfulness, but one of power, love, and sound judgment.

2 Timothy 1:7 HCSB

My cup runs over. Surely goodness and mercy shall follow me all the days of my life; and I will dwell in the house of the Lord Forever.

Psalm 23:5-6 NKJV

I am able to do all things through Him who strengthens me.

Philippians 4:13 HCSB

But if we hope for what we do not see, we eagerly wait for it with patience.

Romans 8:25 HCSB

Lord, I turn my hope to You. My God, I trust in You.

Psalm 25:1-2 HCSB

Make me hear joy and gladness.

Psalm 51:8 NKJV

*Let us hold on to the confession of our hope without wavering,
for He who promised is faithful.*

Hebrews 10:23 HCSB

The following verses remind us that it always pays to obey God.

Who is wise and understanding among you? He should show his works by good conduct with wisdom's gentleness.

James 3:13 HCSB

But whoever keeps His word, truly the love of God is perfected in him. By this we know that we are in Him. He who says he abides in Him ought himself also to walk just as He walked.

1 John 2:5-6 NKJV

For this is what love for God is: to keep His commands. Now His commands are not a burden, because whatever has been born of God conquers the world. This is the victory that has conquered the world: our faith.

1 John 5:3-4 HCSB

You must follow the Lord your God and fear Him. You must keep His commands and listen to His voice; you must worship Him and remain faithful to Him.

Deuteronomy 13:4 HCSB

Because the eyes of the Lord are on the righteous and His ears are open to their request. But the face of the Lord is against those who do evil.

1 Peter 3:12 HCSB

Don't be deceived: God is not mocked. For whatever a man sows he will also reap, because the one who sows to his flesh will reap corruption from the flesh, but the one who sows to the Spirit will reap eternal life from the Spirit.

Galatians 6:7-8 HCSB

Therefore, get your minds ready for action, being self-disciplined, and set your hope completely on the grace to be brought to you at the revelation of Jesus Christ. As obedient children, do not be conformed to the desires of your former ignorance but, as the One who called you is holy, you also are to be holy in all your conduct.

1 Peter 1:13-15 HCSB

Since God rewards kindness just as surely as He punishes cruelty, it always pays to be kind.

Just as you want others to do for you, do the same for them.

Luke 6:31 HCSB

Finally, all of you be of one mind, having compassion for one another; love as brothers, be tenderhearted, be courteous.

1 Peter 3:8 NKJV

Love is patient; love is kind.

1 Corinthians 13:4 HCSB

Pure and undefiled religion before our God and Father is this: to look after orphans and widows in their distress and to keep oneself unstained by the world.

James 1:27 HCSB

And may the Lord make you increase and abound in love to one another and to all.

1 Thessalonians 3:12 NKJV

And be kind and compassionate to one another, forgiving one another, just as God also forgave you in Christ.

Ephesians 4:32 HCSB

Carry one another's burdens; in this way you will fulfill the law of Christ.

Galatians 6:2 HCSB

Be hospitable to one another without complaining.

1 Peter 4:9 HCSB

Don't neglect to show hospitality, for by doing this some have welcomed angels as guests without knowing it.

Hebrews 13:2 HCSB

Whether you're in the garden, in the city, or anyplace in between, it pays to rejoice.

But let all who take refuge in You rejoice.

Psalm 5:11 HCSB

Delight yourself also in the Lord, and He shall give you the desires of your heart.

Psalm 37:4 NKJV

Rejoice in the Lord, you righteous ones; praise from the upright is beautiful.

Psalm 33:1 HCSB

Weeping may endure for a night, but joy comes in the morning.

Psalm 30:5 NKJV

This is the day the Lord has made; let us rejoice and be glad in it.

Psalm 118:24 HCSB

Rejoice in the Lord always. I will say it again: Rejoice!

Philippians 4:4 HCSB

But now I come to You, and these things I speak in the world, that they may have My joy fulfilled in themselves.

John 17:13 NKJV

Rejoice evermore. Pray without ceasing. In every thing give thanks: for this is the will of God in Christ Jesus concerning you.

1 Thessalonians 5:16-18 KJV

Glory in His holy name; let the hearts of those rejoice who seek the Lord! Seek the Lord and His strength; seek His face evermore!

1 Chronicles 16:10-11 NKJV

The following verses remind us that God's Word will endure forever.

Heaven and earth will pass away, but My words will never pass away.

Matthew 24:35 HCSB

But the word of the Lord endures forever. And this is the word that was preached as the gospel to you.

1 Peter 1:25 HCSB

All Scripture is inspired by God and is profitable for teaching, for rebuking, for correcting, for training in righteousness, so that the man of God may be complete, equipped for every good work.

2 Timothy 3:16-17 HCSB

For I am not ashamed of the gospel, because it is God's power for salvation to everyone who believes.

Romans 1:16 HCSB

For the word of God is living and effective and sharper than any two-edged sword, penetrating as far as to divide soul, spirit, joints, and marrow; it is a judge of the ideas and thoughts of the heart.

Hebrews 4:12 HCSB

The one who is from God listens to God's words. This is why you don't listen, because you are not from God.

John 8:47 HCSB

Man shall not live by bread alone, but by every word that proceeds from the mouth of God.

Matthew 4:4 NKJV

MORE FROM GOD'S WORD
GOD'S PLAN

God has a plan for everything, and that includes you.

"For I know the plans I have for you"—[this is] the Lord's declaration—"plans for [your] welfare, not for disaster, to give you a future and a hope."

Jeremiah 29:11 HCSB

We know that all things work together for the good of those who love God: those who are called according to His purpose.

Romans 8:28 HCSB

But as for you, you meant evil against me; but God meant it for good, in order to bring it about as it is this day, to save many people alive.

Genesis 50:20 NKJV

Teach me to do Your will, for You are my God. May Your gracious Spirit lead me on level ground.

Psalm 143:10 HCSB

For My thoughts are not your thoughts, nor are your ways My ways, says the LORD. "For as the heavens are higher than the earth, so are My ways higher than your ways, and My thoughts than your thoughts."

Isaiah 55:8-9 NKJV

A man's heart plans his way, but the Lord directs his steps.

Proverbs 16:9 NKJV

Who is the person who fears the Lord? He will show him the way he should choose. He will live a good life, and his descendants will inherit the land.

Psalm 25:12-13 HCSB

We conclude with verses about Jesus, the Light of the world.

Then He said to them all, "If anyone wants to come with Me, he must deny himself, take up his cross daily, and follow Me."

Luke 9:23 HCSB

Love consists in this: not that we loved God, but that He loved us and sent His Son to be the propitiation for our sins.

1 John 4:10 HCSB

Therefore if any man be in Christ, he is a new creature: old things are passed away; behold, all things are become new.

2 Corinthians 5:17 KJV

Jesus Christ is the same yesterday, today, and forever.

Hebrews 13:8 HCSB

I have come as a light into the world, so that everyone who believes in Me would not remain in darkness.

John 12:46 HCSB

But we do see Jesus—made lower than the angels for a short time so that by God's grace He might taste death for everyone—crowned with glory and honor because of the suffering of death.

Hebrews 2:9 HCSB

For unto us a Child is born, unto us a Son is given; and the government will be upon His shoulder. And His name will be called Wonderful, Counselor, Mighty God, Everlasting Father, Prince of Peace.

Isaiah 9:6 NKJV

In the beginning was the Word, and the Word was with God, and the Word was God . . . . And the Word was made flesh, and dwelt among us, (and we beheld his glory, the glory as of the only begotten of the Father,) full of grace and truth.

John 1:1, 14 KJV

The next day John saw Jesus coming toward him and said, "Here is the Lamb of God, who takes away the sin of the world!

John 1:29 HCSB

A garden teems with life.
It glows with colour and smells like
heaven and puts forward at every
hour of a summer day beauties which
man could never have created and
could not even,
on his own resources, have imagined.

—

C. S. Lewis